MW01137647

The
THOMAS
JAY OORD
Sampler

SacraSage Press

SacraSagePress.com

© 2022 SacraSage Press and Thomas Jay Oord

All rights reserved. No part of this book may be reproduced in any form without written consent of the author or SacraSage Press. SacraSage Press provides resources that promote wisdom aligned with sacred perspectives. All rights reserved.

Interior Design: Nicole Sturk

Front Cover Photo: Thomas Jay Oord

Back Cover Photo: Mark Umstot

Print: 978-1-948609-66-1

Electronic: 978-1-948609-67-8

Printed in the United States of America

Library of Congress Cataloguing-in-Publication Data

The Thomas Jay Oord Sampler / Thomas Jay Oord

.

Note From Thomas Jay Oord

I'm thrilled to join with SacraSage Press to offer this sampling of my writing! I've chosen some of what I consider the best selections, and I hope they whet your appetite for more.

The ideas in this sampling have changed the lives of untold people. I frequently receive social media messages, emails, and letters from readers who witness to the life-changing power of this material. People talk with me after lectures or over coffee and tell personal stories of transformation. I hope these ideas help you too.

I enjoy corresponding with readers. So if you have some insights to share or questions to ask, drop me a line on social media or send me an email: tjoord (at) nnu.edu. I want to hear from you!

Thomas Jay Oord

Samples

OPEN AND RELATIONAL THEOLOGY

AN INTRODUCTION TO LIFE-CHANGING IDEAS

TABLE OF CONTENTS

PREFACE

People across the globe are discovering open and relational theology. The paths leading to this perspective are diverse, and its ideas help many make sense of God, their lives, and our beautiful but sometimes painful world. This book introduces those ideas.

Scholars have explored and promoted the ideas in open and relational theology for decades. Some write books so technical only experts understand them. Others write at a level understood only by graduate students or theology enthusiasts.

This book is different.

I write so that most adults can understand. My goal is to inform and stimulate creative thinking about what matters most.

Some ideas in this book will strike you as radical, unsettling, even mind-blowing. They'll expand your awareness and change your life. I recommend early morning or midnight walks to process them. You'll have a lot to think about!

When most people encounter this theology, they respond, "*Finally!* Something that makes sense!" These ideas align with our deepest intuitions and everyday experiences. They match scripture well, although we must abandon some interpretations people have offered. Other people take longer to "warm up" to these concepts, but they eventually see their winsomeness and wisdom.

New ideas upset the same ol' same ol'. Those who want the status quo find open and relational concepts threatening. I'm among many forced out of faith communities, leadership roles, or teaching positions for embracing these ideas.

A few even scream "heretics" at me and others who accept open and relational thinking. Most who play the heresy card don't know what it means or how heresy charges are rightly decided. I recommend focusing attention on what *actually* matters. We're better off to flee the dogma police than let traditional nonsense keep us from living and thinking well.

A warning: I sometimes write about horrific experiences like rape, death, and torture. I do so, because those are realities in the world. Many books that talk about God ignore the horrors and heartache of life, presenting life as serene and rosy, parroting pat answers too.

Ignoring life's pain comes at a cost: irrelevance. Theology worth embracing must account for beauty and evil, warm fuzzies and intense suffering. But addressing these horrors can trigger some readers. So, I offer this warning.

Introductory books can't cover every topic or go into depth. I encourage readers to explore other open and relational writings. At the conclusion of this book, I offer an abbreviated list of writings and authors published in the last thirty years. I call it "Going Deeper."

I also encourage you to explore the resources at The Center for Open and Relational Theology (c4ort dot com). Sign up for the monthly newsletter while you're on the website and consider adding your voice to the People section. Other fine organizations promote open and relational ideas too, and you'll find links to them on the Center site.

This book can't say everything. It lays out essential ideas in clear and provocative ways. Even the basics of open and relational theology breathe new life into our quest to understand God, make sense of existence, and live well together.

Get ready for an adventure!

1

WHY

MONICA

Monica wishes she could ignore Christmas.

To her, the holiday no longer signifies Jesus' birth or giving gifts. For Monica, Christmas means rape. *Hers*.

For months, the Allenton Baptist Youth Choir spent hour after hour practicing its Christmas Eve musical. The grey church basement echoed as they sang, and while this was not Westminster Cathedral, the acoustics suited them well.

The missing ingredient to the nearly all female choir was some voices to cover the lower registers. So Reverend Sanders convinced Devon and Jaker to join. Both had graduated and had to miss some practices because of work.

Monica felt a spark when Devon walked into the choir room the first time. He walked with confidence and his eyes were shiny and misty all at once. She *liked* him!

In subsequent rehearsals, she would smile shyly or stand near him at breaks. Devon didn't seem to notice... until the last rehearsal. Monica caught him glancing her way during *Silent Night*.

"You should come over," he said after rehearsal. "We need to celebrate."

"Celebrate what?" asked Monica, slightly tilting her head and grinning.

"You know... the season. And no school... whatever," said Devon.

Monica slipped out that evening and walked through Lion's Park to Devon's place. She arrived to find him with Jaker watching the Titans vs. Patriots on Sunday Night Football.

"The others are coming later," Devon said as he let her in. She joined them on the couch watching the Titans lose (again!) and drinking a few beers. After the game, Devon asked Monica if she'd like to go to his room to play *The Last of Us* on his PlayStation. After a while, Jaker joined them.

And that's when it happened. She thought they were just a little too handsy at first. She pushed the two away and struggled; they were stronger. Monica wishes she could forget the rest.

This Christmas, she wonders if God *really* cares. For her. If God loves us enough to send Jesus, why didn't He love her enough to stop her rape?

Monica no longer believes the words, "Emmanuel, God with us."

JIMMY

Campfires have a way of inspiring reflection.

Jimmy organized a "Guys' Weekend" last summer in the Sawtooth Mountains of Idaho. He invited gym buddies and friends from a Bible study, figuring they'd all get along.

"I've been thinking about hell," said Michael as the guys poked at the campfire the first night. "I don't think I believe in it anymore."

"Whatya mean?" someone asked.

"Well... it makes no sense," Michael responded. "Why would a loving God send someone to eternal punishment? In flames bigger than those," he said, gesturing toward the fire. "God's supposed to be loving and fair. The punishment doesn't fit the crime."

After a moment, Hector responded. "I learned about hell at Bishop Kelly High School." Realizing not everyone would understand, he explained: "I was brought up Catholic and went to Catholic schools. I guess I'll always be Catholic."

"Sister Gracie read Dante's *Inferno*," Hector continued. "She showed us paintings of people in fiery caves, twisting in agony. Damned if it didn't scare the hell out of me! Or *into* me!" Hector laughed at his play on words.

"I was raised Baptist," Michael replied. "We didn't have pictures, but preachers described hell: white-hot coals, torture chambers, and laughing demons. I had nightmares! As I got older, talk of hell seemed more like behavior control: 'Don't have sex before you're married, or you'll go to hell.' Of course, that didn't stop me and most guys. Or girls, for that matter!'"

Several smiled and nodded in agreement.

Others joined the conversation. Some said belief in hell was important for curbing crime and resisting temptation. Others said "hell as deterrent" didn't work; people still hurt each other. Besides, a *loving* God wouldn't damn anyone to *everlasting* pain.

Some said actions need consequences. That idea prompted a discussion of God's forgiveness, and someone asked about Hitler. Does a rotten guy like him get off Scot-free? A discussion of discipline ensued. And on it went.

After an hour, Jimmy asked a question. He didn't intend to end the conversation, but his question had that effect.

"Is there a way to believe God always forgives and doesn't send anyone to hell," he asked, "but also that destructive behavior has consequences?"

ROCHELLE

"I'll put that on the prayer chain."

Rochelle heard this phrase often. It's the response her mother gives to news about sickness, job loss, death, accidents, or anything needing prayer. The "prayer chain" rallies "prayer warriors" to "pray down the blessing."

When Rochelle was young, the prayer chain consisted of a written list of phone numbers. Today, mother has gone digital: text messages, Facebook groups, email threads, WhatsApp, and more.

Critics say prayer chains are just church-endorsed gossip, but Rochelle has been pondering bigger questions. She wonders what prayer says about who God is and how God acts.

On their drive home from her sophomore year at Missouri State University, she mustered the courage to start a conversation with her mom.

"I've been trying to make sense of prayer," Rochelle began, "the prayer that asks God to do something."

"What are you thinking?" her mother responded, turning down the Beach Boys.

"Well, God doesn't seem to answer many prayers," said Rochelle. "At least not in tangible ways."

"It happens more than you'd think, Honey," said her mother. "But God's ways are mysterious, and His timing is not ours. You never know how the Lord will answer prayer."

"I guess," said Rochelle, unconvinced. "But do prayers really change what God does? Think about it: wouldn't a loving God help even if we didn't ask? You'd help me if I *really* needed it, right?"

"Yes, I'd help," said her mother. "But it's nice to be asked!"

"I get that," Rochelle said. "Maybe I can explain what I'm thinking by asking some questions."

Rochelle's mother nodded.

"Do you think God knows everything that will ever happen?" asked Rochelle.

"Yes," her mother responded.

"Can God make a mistake about this knowledge?" asked Rochelle. "You know, like God knew you'd never get pregnant, but, Oops! Then you had me?"

Her mother laughed. "God doesn't make mistakes," she said. "If God knows something is true, it's a fact."

"That's the problem," said Rochelle, "if God already knows what will happen in the future and God can't make mistakes, whatever will be, *must* be. It's settled."

"I guess," her mother said.

"When we ask God to do something," said Rochelle, "don't we think the future might be different because we asked? But if God already knows what will happen and can't do other than what He already knows will occur, why pray?"

Her mother sat in silence, eyes fixed on the road as her mind churned through answers. She wanted to believe God knows now all that will happen in the future. And that God can't make mistakes. But she also believed prayer changes things.

"Maybe I can ask it this way," said Rochelle, to break the silence. "Does asking God to fix something change the future... if God already knows what happens in the future?"

KYLER

San Jose has its challenges and opportunities. As the largest city in California's Silicon Valley, its residents know the meaning of change. They also know better than most what it means for people with diverse cultures, economic statuses, IQs, skin colors, and religious beliefs to live together.

Kyler's parents moved to the city early in the dot-com boom. Kyler grew up believing in the power of technology, and he now works at a high-tech company. He married Gary ten years ago, and the two adopted baby girls.

Kyler's been wondering what to teach his daughters about God. His mother was Jewish and his father agnostic, and they taught him the difference between right and wrong. But no one in the family talked about God, at least not seriously. As a result, religious people make Kyler nervous. For his daughters' sake and his own curiosity, however, he's been talking with co-workers about their religious beliefs and commitments.

Steve, a co-worker, has responded to Kyler's inquiries. He's passionate about Christianity and often quotes the Bible and theologians. Steve's been explaining complicated sounding ideas like divine sovereignty, eschatology, and God's hiddenness. Kyler's still confused.

Kyler and Steve stopped for a drink at the Goosetown Lounge after work. Following a little political banter, Kyler said, "I've been thinking about your beliefs and discussing them with Gary. I don't understand the details, but I am trying to make sense of your views."

"Understandable," Steve responded.

"I want to grasp your most important beliefs," Kyler continued. "You know, the forest and not just the trees. And I've got a question."

"Lay it on me," Steve said, focusing his attention.

"In your version of Christianity — 'cuz I know there are many versions — does my life have meaning?"

"Of course!" said Steve, surprised. "The meaning of life is to obey God and enjoy Him forever. That's your purpose. That reminds me," he added, "I need to get you a copy of *The Purpose Driven Life*."

"Okay," said Kyler, "but I don't understand how this fits with God's sovereign plan."

"How so?" asked Steve.

"Well, if God predestines us before time begins, we aren't free. Our lives are predetermined, like the computers at Tech-Pro. Without true freedom, our choices don't matter. And if my choices don't matter, I don't see how my life matters. What I do makes no *ultimate* difference."

"But you *can* be free," said Steve, "when you do God's will. You're free when you do what God ordains."

"You said that earlier," said Kyler, "but it makes no sense to me. You sound like a politician saying the money is here and not here!"

Steve laughed awkwardly.

"Besides," Kyler continued, "I won't teach my daughters God controls them, *but* they're free. I can imagine one of them coming home at 3 a.m. and saying, 'Don't blame me. God predestined me to be late!'"

Steve laughed. "I get it," he said. "It's a mystery. God's ways are not our ways. Unless you're God, you won't understand it."

"Maybe not," said Kyler, "but I'm searching for beliefs that make sense. I can't believe our life has meaning if God predetermined everything."

Steve sat for a moment, thinking. A server brought another Guinness.

"If God pre-decides everything," Kyler concluded, "freedom isn't real."

CHAD AND JENNY

The Covid-19 pandemic crept across the globe in 2020, wreaking havoc. It killed millions, hospitalized tens of millions, and caused widespread suffering. Most viruses contribute to the health and functioning of life on planet earth, but some, like this one, mutate and cause destruction on a grand scale.

I met Chad on Zoom during the pandemic's early months. He was interested in the doctoral program I direct in open and relational theology. It didn't take long for me to realize he was intellectually capable, and I would enjoy working with him.

Most of our conversation focused on the virus and its impact on his life. Chad's wife, Jenny, had died a month earlier from Covid-induced complications. Both Chad and Jenny had been in the hospital with the virus - Chad recovered and walked out, while Jenny did not.

Due to the highly contagious nature of the virus, hospitals quarantined Covid patients, separating them for fear of spreading the virus among visitors, patients, nurses, and doctors. This meant Chad and Jenny were isolated, separated from each other during the last days of Jenny's life. Chad never got the chance to say goodbye to his best friend and lifelong partner. None of their family could visit or say goodbye either. Jenny died alone.

As we chatted, Chad was reeling. He wept as he talked about his frustrations trying to arrange a funeral during a pandemic. And about loneliness. Chad was hoping the doctoral program might give his life direction now that Jenny was gone. He needed something.

Chad asked the same question hundreds of millions of people across the world asked in 2020 and beyond: "Why didn't God stop Covid-19?"

One poll says two-thirds of American Christians believe the pandemic is God telling humanity to change. Does that make sense? Did God send or allow the coronavirus to teach us a lesson? Are Jenny and millions of dead people changing their ways? And is Chad better off lonely? And what about those still suffering the long-term effects of the virus, causing mental ailments, disabilities, and loss of quality of life?

Wouldn't a loving God prevent needless suffering and death?

A BETTER WAY

This book offers *actual* answers to these questions.

In the following chapters, I explain how open and relational ideas make sense of God's love in light of Monica's questions about rape, campfire questions about hell, Rochelle's questions about prayer, Kyler's questions about free will and meaning, the questions millions of people ask about God and Covid-19, and more.

Without believable answers to life's pressing questions, theology is of little use. God becomes like a pepper shaker: sometimes you sprinkle a bit, but the food tastes fine without it. Why believe in God if belief doesn't matter?

Fortunately, there is another—and a better—way to think.

SURVEY

Two sociologists asked Americans what they believe about God. These scientists interviewed thousands of subjects and consulted surveys from others to learn which theological beliefs are most common. The project results surprised many.

According to their findings, 95% of Americans believe in God. That's more than what many experts thought, but the sociologists define God broadly enough to allow for greater buy-in.[1] Americans have God on their minds.

Most interesting to me were the particular views Americans have about God — what God is like, whether God acts or relates, where God is, God's attitudes, and so on.[2] Survey results show most Americans believe God is 1) Authoritative, 2) Benevolent, 3) Distant, or 4) Critical.[3]

Let's look at each.

An Authoritative God

Almost a third of Americans see God as the cosmic authority. For ease of reference, let's call those who see God this way, "Authoritatives." In this perspective, God is a judge who engages the world and punishes when people do wrong. An authoritative God needs nothing from creatures because that deity is entirely independent.

Authoritatives are more likely than others to think God is a literal father, wrathful, and one who uses pain to discipline. Their rationale comes from Bible stories, the Qur'an, and popular views about punishing those who commit crimes.[4]

Those who see God like this feel compelled to keep rules and want others to do the same. They value allegiance to leadership, commitment to the tribe, and personal responsibility. Loyalty is a top priority for Authoritatives. They believe we can have absolute certainty about what God wants for us and others.[5]

To simplify, Authoritatives believe in a sovereign Judge who punishes the disobedient. In the words of an old song, "Trust and obey, 'cause there's no other way."

A Benevolent God

Most Americans, no matter what model of God they embrace, believe God is loving. Some who see God this way — let's call them "Nurturants," because "Benevolents" is awkward — understand divine love differently than others.[6]

Nurturants make up about a fourth of the American population. They see God's love as constantly forgiving and consoling. God has moral standards but doesn't retaliate against those who do not meet them. Instead, God warns us about the negative consequences that come from sin. The Nurturant perspective sees God as assisting, healing, inspiring, and showing compassion.

The way Authoritatives and Nurturants think about God corresponds with what each considers effective parenting. Nurturants prioritize empathy and care. They value acceptance, cooperation, and taking the perspectives of others. Nurturant parents value free expression from their children but think moral guidelines help kids discern which expressions are positive. Authoritatives think good parenting is strict, demanding, and includes swift punishment.

Nurturants see God as empathetic and forgiving. They embrace "care and share."

A Distant God

Researchers used "Distant" to describe the God in whom about a fourth of Americans believe. This God is not active in the world, nor does He judge the deeds of moral creatures. Believers in a distant God rarely speak of miracles and think biblical stories should never be taken literally. According to researchers, many who initially described themselves as agnostic actually believe in a God who is distant.[7]

Let's call people who believe God is distant and nonjudgmental the "Permissives." A Permissive perspective sees life as having few or no boundaries, standards, or restrictions. Some Permissives advocate extreme tolerance and verge toward anarchy. Others emphasize the liberty to do what an individual desires.

Permissive parents set few limits, not wanting to impose standards and expectations. They value autonomy in their children. Permissives seek to tear down oppressive religious and political systems but offer little or nothing to replace them.

Permissives say God exists, and just about anything goes.

A Critical God

The least common perspective of God among Americans (16%) says deity does not engage creation but keeps track of what we do. The Critical God will judge us after we die according to what we do here and now. Although responsible for moral standards and the regularities in the universe, this God doesn't intervene in earthly affairs.

As one disengaged, the Critical God is unaffected by what happens in our lives or the world. God has no emotions and can't feel pain or joy. We see the handiwork of this God in the design of a universe created long ago in some way we cannot describe.

Once we perish, the Critical God rewards the righteous and makes evildoers pay. This punishment might be eternal torment, purgatory, or annihilation. The reward for the righteous is eternal bliss on streets of gold or orgies with a thousand virgins. While the Critical God doesn't punish or reward now, this deity enforces the consequences later.[8]

The Critical God, like Santa Claus, is making a list and checking it twice to judge who's naughty or nice.

CERTAINTY

So… what is the correct view? Which model gets God *right*?

That's impossible to know with certainty. Scholars like myself analyze details in these and other models. We break them into sub-models and those into sub-sub-models. And then argue about minutiae.

I believe an open and relational view of God makes the most sense overall. But I'm not certain. I don't know God fully, so I can't be 100% sure. I look at reality through limited and sometimes distorted lenses, which means my vision is cloudy.

I just don't know for sure.

Open and relational thinkers can't *prove* their view is the right one. Theological statements like "God loves us" aren't mathematical equations like $2 + 2 = 4$. They're not verifiable statements like we say, "Jesse Owens won 4 gold medals in the 1936 Olympics."

No person — theist, atheist, or agnostic — has perfect vision of ultimate reality. We all wear distorted lenses.

Those who think they've figured out God are closed. Like a ship come to port, they've "arrived" at a secure harbor with nothing more to learn. The rest of us continue searching, sailing the waters of life. We're open.

Searching doesn't mean we're fumbling about with no sense of direction whatsoever. We can both search and be on a journey that makes sense, gives joy, and contributes to living well. We can find an escapade of significance between utter ignorance and absolute certainty.

To put it bluntly: some portrayals of God *are* better than others. Some are more plausible, for instance. Some portrayals account for the universe better. For our experiences better. Scriptures better or science better. Our intuitions or aesthetics better. And so on.

When it comes to God, we can't be certain. But we aren't clueless.

CONVENTIONAL THEOLOGY

On my way to explaining open and relational theology, it might help to identify theologies that are *unlike* it. You know, the alternatives. We can learn a lot about a view if we know what it opposes.

To avoid getting lost in the weeds, I'll use the label, "conventional God" for a host of views open and relational thinkers oppose. Under this label rests a potpourri of problematic ideas. I suspect you'll recognize many, others may surprise you.

Millions of people believe in the conventional God I describe below, and we could point to thousands of nuances within this perspective. Painting a general portrait is sufficient for the contrast I offer throughout this book.

Here are key features of the conventional God...

The conventional God exists above or outside time. Watching from this external perspective, He knows all that has ever happened and everything that will happen as if it already occurred. He's more like an abstract number than a loving sister; more like a definition than a person. The future is settled for this God in the same way the past is settled. And yes, the conventional God is usually thought of as masculine.

Call Him "the timeless God."

The conventional God is unaffected by what we do. Creation makes no difference to Him, because He can't be influenced. The conventional God never has a change of mind or alters course in response to creation, because creatures have no effect on Him. This God can't be compassionate in any sense that we understand compassion, because such love requires a response. Despite what people say, the unaffected God can't really respond to prayer.

Call Him "the uninfluenced God."

This God is in control. By either manipulating every creature in every instant or manipulating only those moments He deems important, the conventional God orchestrates history to a predetermined end. This means God either causes or permits all evil. The Nazi Holocaust? God did it or permitted it. Your cousin's car accident? God could have stopped it but chose not to. Child abuse? This God allows that too. The conventional God is large and in charge.

Call Him "the controlling God."

This God is pristine. He can't be in the presence of unholy creatures like you and me. We are dirty rotten scoundrels wallowing in the pit of sinful despair. To overcome this problem, the conventional God had to kill His Son. He now sees us through the lens of this atoning death and thinks we're pure when we aren't.

Call Him "the ultimate Germaphobe," and we're the germs.

The conventional God usually keeps a distance, preoccupied with His own glory. He's a lot like a narcissist. When necessary, He'll intervene to fiddle with creation or barge in where not welcome. The conventional God usually works through the laws of nature and natural systems He installed singlehandedly.

He occasionally breaks those laws and systems if it's important enough.

Call Him "the intervening God."

Our actions don't make a difference to the future the conventional God already knows as fact. He knows who ends up in heaven and who will fry in hell. We can't alter a future this God knows as settled and complete, because to alter it would make Him a liar. What we think are the beginning and end are a single moment to the conventional God.

Call Him "the foreknowing God."

The conventional God loves some people, sometimes. Maybe. Mostly He's mad, pissed at deplorable sinners who dare to disobey. This God usually punishes the unrepentant promptly, but on a good day, He may show a hand of mercy. Like the Roman emperor whose thumbs up or down depends on his own mood, you hope the conventional God is in a good mood. Don't count on forgiveness, because the conventional God can do whatever He damn well pleases. And "damning" is what He does well.

Call Him "the angry God."

I could identify more characteristics, but this should suffice. This vision of God sounds familiar to most people. It may sound familiar to you.

I don't believe in this God.

UNSATISFYING

Conventional theologies take various forms and have subtle nuances. I don't want to give the impression everyone who accepts the conventional model is unintelligent or naïve. Intellectually sophisticated versions of these ideas exist. But even the most sophisticated conventional descriptions do not convince me and others. Sometimes, the sophisticated versions are *especially* unsatisfying.

Did you notice some features of the conventional God contradict one another? God is said to be both angry at creatures and uninfluenced by them, for instance. If creatures can't influence God, how could they make Him angry? Or God is both timeless but also intervening. To intervene implies a time sequence in which God had not intervened and then did. Or God is both controlling but unable to be in our presence. How can an absent God control us?

Some conventional theologies correct these inconsistencies by choosing one feature and setting aside the other. This doesn't alleviate the problems, of course. Eliminating half a contradiction can make it more obvious just how bad the remaining problem is.

Other conventional theologies accept the inconsistencies and appeal to mystery, saying finite minds can't understand an infinite God. This kind of mystery helps no one. In fact, it adds another problem: unintelligibility. We end up with a schizophrenic God who is timeless but intervening, angry but uninfluenced, and controlling but not around.

Unintelligible!

Did you also notice the conventional view aligns most with the Authoritative and Critical models of God we looked at earlier? More than half of Americans embrace those views, and I suspect they dominate much of the world. The conventional view of God has deep, long-lasting, and worldwide influence.

It's time for something better.

NOT YOUR BOYFRIEND

Open and relational theology also comes in many forms. There's no one mold or type, no uniform vision everyone must embrace. Among the four models of God presented by sociologists, open and relational theology comes closest to the Benevolent/Nurturant view.[9] In fact, it's common for open and relational thinkers to start with "God is love" as they consider theology, their lives, and existence.

When asked, *most* people say God is loving. Eighty-five percent of Americans said so, according to the research. When many — especially theologians — explain what they mean by divine love, the God they describe sounds like a jerk! (Crass synonyms for "jerk" were in this book's earlier drafts.)

For instance, the God of conventional theologies has no emotions and feels nothing. He's apathetic, and that's just the start. The conventional God sends people to eternal torment, plays favorites, might choose to stop loving us, controls others, lashes out in vengeance, considers humans deplorable, and allows rape, genocide, and torture. (See why "jerk" isn't strong enough!)

The God of conventional theology is a Controlling Boyfriend in the Sky. Who'd want to spend eternity with Him?!

APPEALING REASONS

Open and relational theology understands God differently.

I'll explain the differences in coming chapters. Before we look at them, it helps to know *why* many people are attracted to open and relational thinking.

Below, in no particular order, are reasons many find open and relational theology appealing...

Answers Big Questions

A good number of open and relational thinkers arrived at these ideas after an intellectual quest. Some wrestled for years with questions about divine grace and sovereignty. Others wondered about God's relation to time and the future. Some looked for a solution to why a loving and powerful God doesn't prevent evil — "Why do bad things happen to good people?" Some wanted to harmonize science and religion. Others tried to reconcile their sense of free will with a powerful God active in their lives. Some looked for a theology that didn't imply God is an old white guy mansplaining morality. And many other questions that arise. Open and relational theology offers solutions to life's big questions.

Scripture

Open and relational thinkers believe sacred scriptures point to the primacy of divine love. Jews (and Christians) highlight the fifteen times the following words appear in the Hebrew Bible: "The Lord is compassionate and gracious, slow to act in anger, abounding in lovingkindness, and forgiving iniquity and transgression.[10]" Muslims build a case for open and relational theology from the Qur'an. "Allah is the ultimate source of instant beneficence and eternal mercy," the scriptures begin, "who encompasses the entire universe.[11]" Christians might emphasize "God is love"[12] and such other passages in the New Testament. God as described in most scripture makes sense in an open and relational framework.[13]

Logic of Love

Other advocates of open and relational theology start with the logic of love itself, irrespective of what any sacred book might say. They ask questions like: Does love cause or allow unnecessary pain? Does love predestine some to eternal hell? Does love control others? Does love concern itself only with self-interest? Does love make sense without freedom? To each of these questions open and relational thinkers answer, "No!" The logic of love leads to believing a loving God is open and relational.

Intuitions

Others come to open and relational theology by following their deepest intuitions. They may not have been exposed to any religion or have even rejected every religion, but they respond to truth, beauty, and goodness. A Source grounds and summons such responses. If this Source is loving, it must be relational rather than static, engaging an open future and not a settled one. The deep intuitions of many fit the open and relational vision.

Social Sciences

Another entryway to open and relational thinking starts by asking, "What if we took seriously research on relationships in psychology, sociology, communications, and medicine?" Then one asks, "What if we believed God relates in the ways this research says healthy people relate?" Studies suggest we're healthier when not manipulated, bullied, neglected, or abused. We are healthier when we're not doing the manipulating, etc. People who think God nurtures and who imitate that version of God have, on average, better relationships, greater psychological well-being, and more positive social connections. Some embrace what social science tells us about the good life and extrapolate what this means about God.

Relational Reality

Others have come to open and relational theology not so much to find answers but because it fits the way they naturally relate. This is a common entryway for some feminists, for instance. A relational God who engages noncoercively fits what many intuit is the best way to get along in the world. It fits existence top to bottom, simple to complex, individual to community. If we are open and relational beings in an open and relational world, why not think our Creator is open and relational?

Jesus

Many Christians point to Jesus as the primary reason they embrace open and relational theology. In their eyes, the persuasive love of Jesus — who re-presents God[14] — reveals God as one who loves nonviolently. Jesus engaged in giving and receiving love with others, believing their responses were not predetermined.

We best know what God's love is, say some, from the life, teachings, sufferings, death, and resurrection of Jesus.[15] Open and relational theology offers a framework to make sense of God in light of Jesus.

Science and Philosophy

Still others follow theories in science and philosophy to an open and relational view. Most physicists, biologists, and chemists find creation to be evolving and expanding. Some propose that a God who also evolves and expands must have created it. To make sense of morality and existence, many ethicists and metaphysicians propose the existence of an open and relational deity who grounds morals and calls existence toward complexity. A large percentage of scholars exploring issues in science and religion embrace an open and relational perspective.

The Perfect Being

One might come to believe God is open and relational through what some call "Perfect Being" theology. Instead of starting with scripture, science, religious experience, philosophies, or wisdom traditions, this approach asks, "What would a perfect being be like?" This perfect being is, of course, what many call God. If love is the greatest among divine perfections, one might deduce that a loving God is perfectly open and relational. Beginning with love overcomes contradictions in theologies that instead start with divine omnipotence, timelessness, or changeless perfection.

Artistic Sensibility

Artists and the artistically minded find open and relational theology attractive for how it fits their vision of the creative life.
Imagining a new form of being or way of thinking fits nicely with
a theology that says God acts in fresh ways and inspires novelty
in creation. It would make sense that both the Supreme Artist
and creaturely artists create in relation to objects and their own
sparks of originality.

Meaning and Purpose

I conclude with a final reason some find open and relational
theology appealing. The open and relational view provides a
framework for thinking our lives have meaning and purpose.
Most theologies portray God as one who pre-programs life or
can get results singlehandedly. In those theologies, our choices
can't ultimately matter. By contrast, open and relational thinking says we have genuinely free choices. Not even God can stop
us. Because the future rests, in part, on what we decide, our lives
have meaning and purpose.

These are some reasons a growing number of people find open
and relational theology attractive. They build from diverse ways
of living and thinking.

It's time to dump that Controlling Boyfriend in the Sky.

QUESTIONS:

1. Which questions in the five opening stories are most relevant to you? To which do you relate most?
2. What is the biggest question you have about who God is and how God acts?
3. Are you surprised by the research results describing models of God embraced by Americans? If so, what surprises you? If not, why not?
4. What aspects of the conventional God do you find puzzling, troubling, or unappealing? Give an example of a situation in which the conventional view of God influenced how people acted.
5. Which of the reasons many people find open and relational theology attractive do you find intriguing?

Scan the QR code for a video interview on God and the Covid-19 pandemic.

ENDNOTES

1. WHY

1. Paul Froese and Christopher Bader, *America's Four Gods: What We Say About God — and What That Says About Us* (Oxford: Oxford University Press, 2010) 4, 149.

2. To my knowledge, it remains largely unstudied how people in other countries think about God — at least in terms of these categories. I suspect there are surprising similarities and interesting differences.

3. The percentages: Authoritative (32%), Benevolent (24%), Distant (24%), and Critical (16%). See chapter one in See chapter one in *America's Four Gods*.

4. Ibid., 28-29.

5. For deeper exploration of how views of God correspond with values and orientations in life, see John Sanders, *Embracing Prodigals: Overcoming Authoritative Religion by Embodying Jesus' Nurturing Grace* (Eugene, OR: Cascade, 2020). Sanders cites psychological and sociological studies in his book.

6. Froese and Bader, *America's Four Gods*, 15.

7. Ibid., 35.

8. Ibid., 32.

9. On this, see John Sanders, *Embracing Prodigals*.

10. Exod 34:6-7; etc.

11. *Qu'ran* 1:1-3.

12. 1 Jn 4:8,16.

13. Note to fellow Christians with a high view of the Bible: I could have written this book and profusely peppered it with biblical passages. I think the Bible strongly supports an open and relational view, although I admit some passages have been interpreted in ways that fit conventional theology. I chose not to cite the Bible frequently (although I do occassionally), because I want to appeal to those without much knowledge of scripture. I also write to those burnt-out or even abused by those who, often with good intentions, have used the Bible more as a weapon than as medicine. To go deeper on the ways the Bible supports an open and relational perspective, consult the books and authors I mention in the "Going Deeper" section of this book.

14. Heb. 1:3.

15. 1 John 3:16.

For the remainder of the book, visit your favorite bookseller...

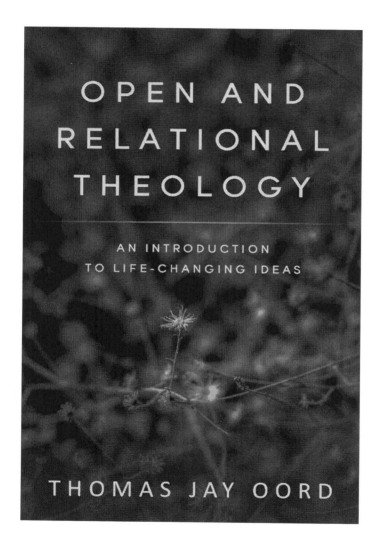

God Can't!

How to Believe in God and Love
after Tragedy, Abuse, or Other Evils

Table of Contents

A Solution to Evil

A Solution to Evil

The Las Vegas Strip was packed and buzzing. Nearly 20,000 people milled about the Route 91 Harvest Festival that October night, singing with country music star Jason Aldean, the festival's final performer.

High above the crowd, a 64-year-old former auditor, Stephen Paddock, looked down from the Mandalay Bay Hotel. He visited Vegas often, living eighty miles northeast of the city, and casino hosts knew him by name.

Placing "Do Not Disturb" signs on adjacent rooms, the ex-auditor moved to the windows of the hotel's thirty-second floor, smashed them with a hammer, and began spraying bullets into the crowd below.

In the next ten minutes, Paddock pulled the triggers of twenty guns and fired at least 1,100 rounds. Fifty-eight people died; 851 were injured. Thousands of survivors are traumatized long after the deadliest mass shooting by an individual in the United States.

Many asked questions in the aftermath. Where was God? Why didn't God stop the massacre? And does it make sense to believe God cares for *everyone*?

Many people think God had the power to prevent the Las Vegas shooting, its deaths, injuries, and resulting trauma. They think God could have warned officials, temporarily paralyzed the gunman, jammed the rifles, or redirected every bullet flying 400 yards. They assume God has the ability to do just about anything.

After the shooting, some "explained" why God failed to stop the tragedy. "There's a higher purpose in this," they said. Others appealed to mystery: "We just can't understand God's ways."

The president of the Southern Baptist Ethics and Religious Liberty Commission, Russell Moore, captured the thoughts of many. "We do not know why God does not intervene and stop some tragedies when he does stop others," said Moore. "What we do know, though, is that God stands against evil and violence. We know that God is present for those who are hurting."[1]

Really?

If God stands against evil and violence, why doesn't God stop them? Does God's desire to be "present for those who are hurting" trump God's desire to protect? Does God allow death and injury because He's needy, desperate for attention, or wanting to feel useful?

Where is God in the midst of tragedy, abuse, and other evil?

THIS BOOK
Life can wound, abuse, cut, and destroy. I'm not talking about a bad day at the office or a Facebook argument. And I'm not just

talking about horrors like the Las Vegas shooting. I'm talking about genuine evil of various kinds: rape, betrayal, genocide, theft, abuse, cancer, slander, torture, murder, corruption, incest, disease, war, and more.

Sensible people admit evil occurs. Survivors know the pain personally.

I wrote this book for victims of evil, survivors, and those who endure senseless suffering. I wrote it for the wounded and broken who have trouble believing in God, are confused, or have given up faith altogether. I'm writing to those who, like me, are damaged in body, mind, or soul.

This book is also for those who don't call themselves "victims" or "survivors" but have been wronged. They may not call what happened "evil," but they hurt. These people wonder what God was doing when they were betrayed, personally attacked, or unjustly laid off work. Where was God when they struggled through divorce, had miscarriages, were cheated, suffered prolonged illness, or had a freak accident?

In light of suffering, we ask challenging questions and seek believable answers. We want to make sense of evil, love, freedom, pain, randomness, healing ... and God.

We want to understand.

You and I aren't the first to ask these questions. But the answers you'll get in this book are different from what you've heard. It's a safe bet, in fact, this book's ideas will change you. You'll think differently.

I say this as a theologian, clergy, and scholar of multi-disciplinary studies who trained at leading institutions

The answers in this book are different from those you've heard.

of higher education and lectured in prestigious universities on nearly every continent. I also say this as someone who engages people in small, out-of-the-way communities among the everyday living of down-to-earth folk.

I spend most of my time exploring the big issues of life; I care about what matters most. This means drawing from science, philosophy, spirituality, and religion.[2] It means looking carefully at day-to-day life, both the ordinary and extraordinary. My experiences with diverse people tell me the ideas in this book will not only strike you as unusual, they'll change the way you think and live.

I wrote this book for you.

Our stories — yours and mine — matter. They portray the reality of our lived experience. We must face reality with clear-eyed honesty if we want to heal, love, and believe. Being honest about the past can open us to a better future.

I tell true stories in this book. But I sometimes change the names of survivors and details of their stories to protect their identities. You probably know similar stories. Perhaps your story sounds like one I describe.

A word to the conventional, play-it-safe reader: you probably won't like this book. You'll think these ideas are too radical, too mind blowing, too audacious. You probably won't understand that taking evil seriously means rethinking conventional ideas about God and the world. This book may infuriate you!

Taking evil seriously means rethinking conventional ideas about God and the world.

This book is for survivors... those who hurt... those who care... those who want to make sense of life... and those who want to heal. It's for those who want to love, to be loved, and to live a life of love.

MY FRIENDS ARE HURTING

Survivors tell painful stories derived from personal experience. Listening to them helps us understand suffering better. Their pain is often not just physical or emotional. It also includes confusion, hopelessness, and anger at God.

Our stories point to what hangs in the balance: the nature of love, belief in God, and the meaning of life. There are no higher stakes!

When we take survivors seriously, we take the questions of existence seriously. Finding answers requires wrestling with what life is really like: good and bad. Pretending isn't helpful; we want and need the truth.

There aren't enough books to record every experience of tragedy, abuse, and evil. But I want to tell the stories of four friends. Their experiences help us focus on what's at stake.

Teri - It started in Sunday school. Teri's teacher started touching her. His orange-red mustache quivered as he fondled her body, and to this day, she shudders when she sees a mustache of that color. His fondling led to rubbing. That led to more.... But she doesn't like to talk about it.

Teri is a #MeToo survivor.

During and long after the nightmare her abuser orchestrated, Teri lived in shame. She asked the questions many survivors ask. What's wrong with me? Is this my fault? Should I tell someone? Will anyone want me now? Is life worth living?

She also asked questions of faith: Where is God? Doesn't God care? If God loves me, why didn't He stop this?

It's not surprising Teri lost faith in men. In her mind, they were interested only in their own pleasure. It's also little surprise that Teri has trouble believing in God. Her Sunday school teacher said God was king, the authority to obey, the one in ultimate control.

> "If God loves me, why didn't He stop this?"

If God exists, Teri assumes her abuse is part of some awful plan. Or perhaps she's not on His radar. God's definitely not delivering her from evil, as the Lord's Prayer says.

If God exists, he has an orange-red mustache.

James - As long as he can remember, James struggled with depression. In periods of personal darkness, he could not leave bed. His hair fell out and his weight ballooned. His thoughts fluttered from anger to apathy to suicide.

James tried therapy and medication. He fasted and prayed. His family did their best to love and support him, but depression followed him relentlessly.

James knew the Bible better than most. He'd memorized countless verses, and he taught his children to trust the "good book." While he never seriously doubted the Bible or God, he did have questions.

"Why is this happening to me?" James asked one afternoon over coffee. Was he paying the consequences of sin? Was this his parents' fault? Was his brain damaged in a way God wouldn't heal? Why did God *allow* depression?

An inquisitive mind led James to questions the less courageous dare not ask.

After Christmas last year, James drove to a lake, put a shotgun to his head, and pulled the trigger. The coroner said he died instantly. A hunter found him in his blood-splashed pickup.

"Does God allow depression?"

James's family now asks me the questions he'd been asking. Why didn't God intervene? Couldn't God have jammed the shotgun and prevented this atrocity? Is depression a disease God will not heal?

James's wife asked me a particularly difficult question. "If God has a plan for everyone, was suicide His plan for James? If God doesn't want suicide," she wondered, "why didn't He stop it?"

Maria - Maria and Ted desperately want children. Maria's been doing the right things to make it happen. She cares for her body, watches her diet, and makes healthy choices. She takes vitamins and sees specialists but cannot carry a child full term.

Maria's third miscarriage was especially awful. On that day, she sat on the toilet and cried for an hour. Ted found her after coming home from work. He lay on the bathroom floor, curled up in a ball, and sobbed too.

The people at their church offer plenty of explanations. "The demons are interfering," said one elderly man. "You're demon possessed."

An elder said God allowed miscarriages to make Maria a better person. "God never gives us more than we can handle," he said, "and this will help you mature." According to him, mis-carriages were a divine strategy for building Maria's character.

This alleged divine plan did not work: Maria resents God and she despises church. Maria grows bitter not better.

"I guess there's a God, but who really knows?"

Maria and Ted stopped attending church. Maria still believes in God, mostly because she was raised that way. But she has no idea how God acts. In fact, she's got no clue what God is like. It's a mystery.

"I guess there's a God," she said to me recently. "But who really knows?"

Although Maria believes in God intellectually, it doesn't affect how she actually lives. She's got no idea what God does.

Mysteries don't help Maria.

Rashad - One Friday afternoon as a tenth-grader, Rashad came home to find his father vomiting blood on his black-and-white checkered shirt. A few trips to the doctor confirmed the family's fear: cancer. About a month later, he died.

During that month, everyone prayed. Rashad, his father, the family, their pastor, and friends. The holiest saints prayed, fully believing God heals. The family tried every ritual: anointing with oil, fasting, baptism, and healing ceremonies.

The faithful showed no lack of faith.

At the funeral, Rashad heard an array of "answers" for why his father died. "God's ways are not our ways," said some. "Who are we to question God?" "Give thanks in all things," said others, "God is in control." "We need evil to realize we need salvation." And "Everything happens for a reason."

In the years that followed, the family suffered emotionally, financially, and spiritually. Rashad grew timid and insecure. He mired in crippling uncertainty.

"If this is what God wants," Rashad said one day, "to hell with God! He may be strong, but He isn't good. He's a mean ole' son-of-a-bitch!"

Rashad had been taught that God was a loving Father. But I'll never forget the question he asked, "What kind of parent allows his child to suffer just to teach him to seek help... help from the parent who allowed the suffering in the first place? That's not the logic of love," Rashad said, "that's manipulation."

> *"If this is what God wants, to hell with God!"*

"If God allows evil He could have stopped, we don't need Him," Rashad said. "We need the Child Welfare Agency!"

ANOTHER ANGEL IN HEAVEN'S CHOIR?

These stories are a tiny sample from millions, perhaps billions of similar ones. The attempts in them to explain God's relation to evil are typical. None satisfy.

When we encounter evil, it's natural to ask questions: Why would God cause or allow it? Is God punishing me? If God loves everyone, why doesn't God prevent pointless pain? Does God care? Are God's ways a complete mystery?

I'm not satisfied by the conventional answers: "God needed another angel in heaven's choir," "It's all part of God's plan," "God wants to make you stronger," "God's ways are not our ways." "You didn't have enough faith," "Everything happens for a reason," and more.

Well-meaning people say these things, and I'm not questioning their motives. But these answers don't make sense.

Some include truth, but none satisfy entirely. Appeals to mystery are especially useless.

We need believable answers to the biggest questions of our lives.

In response to bad answers, some turn to atheism. I understand that. Given the evil in the world, some people no longer believe a loving and powerful God exists. And that makes a certain degree of sense. In fact, polls indicate the existence of evil is the number-one reason atheists cite for rejecting belief in God. Who can blame them?

Others continue believing but grow timid, insecure, and fearful. They cannot live with confidence. Some think God is punishing them. Others think God has abandoned them, being concerned with more pressing matters. Many believe in God intellectually but are atheists practically: what they believe doesn't affect how they live.

More than a few people stop searching for an answer. They play the mystery card. In fact, some scoff at attempts to solve the riddle of why a good and powerful God doesn't prevent evil.

FIVE PARTS OF A REAL ANSWER

I think there's a better way. There's a solution to evil that makes sense.

This better way begins with believing in a God of relentless love. It makes sense of tragedy and abuse without saying God caused or even allowed them.

The better way builds on five ideas about God, creation, and evil. Together, they form a solution to why evil occurs and a loving God doesn't stop it. And they give a framework to live well and think clearly.

I reveal these ideas in this book. They *solve* the problem of evil.

Notice I said, "Solve." I didn't say, "We just can't understand God." Not, "You can't prove God *doesn't* exist, so I keep believing despite having no answer for evil." I don't avoid the hard questions and I won't give standard answers.

A real solution.

When taken together, these five ideas direct us to live with zest. Together, they provide the framework to reconstruct mind, body, and soul.

Five ideas provide the solution to why evil occurs and a loving God doesn't stop it.

GOD ALWAYS LOVES

The big ideas in this book share two assumptions, and I want to mention them before going further. The first is that God loves us all, all the time. God loves everyone and everything, all creatures great and small. God never stops loving, even for one moment, because God's nature is love. God listens, feels, and responds by acting for good.

God wills our well-being, not our woe being.

The standard answers to evil often don't portray God as loving, at least not what we consider "loving." Some assume God's love is altogether different from ours. The phrase, "God's ways are not our ways," is taken to mean, "God's love isn't like ours." What God thinks loving is not what we think. This sleight-of-hand confuses rather than clarifies.

It doesn't help to say God loves us if we have no idea what love is!

Other answers assume God allows harm for some greater purpose. When victims suffer, some people say, "God's love is sometimes rough and tough!" "You've got to go through hell before you get to heaven." Or "God knows what's best, so your rape (or some other evil) must be good."

Unfortunately, most people think God causes or allows evil.

If divine love does evil, we should resist it! If God's love allows rape and torture, nobody should want God to love them. Such "love" is no love at all!

By contrast, I believe what God thinks is loving matches what we think is loving. Our intuitions of love fit God's view of love. We best define this shared meaning when love is understood as acting intentionally, in response to God and others, to promote overall well-being. In short, love aims to do good. That view of love applies to Creator and creatures.

God *always* loves, and God's love is *always* good. Every idea I advocate in this book assumes God is loving.

GENUINE EVIL OCCURS

The five ideas in this book also assume evil is real. Some suffering, destruction, and harm are unnecessary. Some pain is pointless. Genuine evil makes the world, all things considered, worse than it might have been.

I'm not saying all pain is bad. We sometimes choose pain for our good or we self-sacrifice for the good of others. But sometimes pain and suffering are useless, and that's what I mean by "genuine evil." Genuinely evil events cause more harm than the good that could have occurred otherwise.

Many answers to questions of pain and suffering don't consider evil genuine. They say, for instance, God allows pain and suffering for some greater good. In this view, the malevolence of the past is required for the beneficence of the future. Or at least God thinks it's better to allow horrors and holocausts than to prevent them.

If God has allowed all past abuse, pain, and suffering for some greater good, nothing has ever occurred that God considers *genuinely* evil. God must have permitted *every* rape, torture, betrayal, murder, deception, corruption, incest, and genocide as part of some good plan. From this twisted perspective, evil is good!

I can't believe that. Neither can most survivors I know. We can't believe *all* abuse, pain, and tragedy are necessary. Not everything happens or is allowed for some divinely appointed reason.

It doesn't make sense to say a loving God *permits* evil. We don't need to say, "Your rape happened for a reason," and mean, "God allowed it." We don't need to believe God allows children to be tortured or think God permits cancer. And so on. We can believe painful experiences and horrific tragedies make the world worse than it might have been. And God didn't want them.

> *It doesn't make sense to say a loving God permits evil.*

Ultimately, evil is evil … from God's perspective and ours.

HOW TO READ THIS BOOK

No one of the five ideas in this book is satisfying on its own. But together they provide a solution to why a loving and powerful God doesn't stop evil. They provide a way toward healing, love, and transformation. Together, they give life!

Because all five play an essential role, don't stop reading partway through this book. If you do, you won't see clearly how you can believe in God and love again. You'll miss the big picture.

Take time to consider each idea carefully. Read slowly. I provide questions for each chapter to help process the proposals. Discuss them with others, or meditate alone with a journal.

New ideas need time to permeate our minds, mend our bodies, and help us live well.

While no other book provides this five-fold solution, some address one or more of the ideas. I list some resources online at GodCant.com, and I update those resources. Look for reminders of the site at the conclusion of each chapter, and explore those resources when you have time.

Remember: the five ideas work well when taken together. We need to see the whole to move toward wholeness.

FOR YOU

If you're a survivor, someone who cares about survivors, or want to answer one of life's biggest questions — why God doesn't prevent evil — this book is for you.

If you want to believe in God — a God of love, not some bully in the sky or absentee parent — this book is for you.

Prepare to reconstruct.

If you want to heal, to hope, and to love, this book is for you.

Prepare to reconstruct.

Questions

1. What answers have you heard for why God causes or allows evil? What do you think of them?

2. What experiences of evil — personal or public — have shaped your view of God?

3. Why do some people think all evil is necessary for some greater good?

4. Why does it matter that what God considers loving matches what we consider loving?

5. Why should we think some pain and suffering is unnecessary or pointless?

6. Is it easy for you to believe God is always good? Why or why not?

7. What question do you hope this book will answer?

CHAPTER ONE

God Can't Prevent Evil

Let me get right to the first idea we need: God can't prevent abuse, tragedy, and evil. You read it right: God *can't.*

A loving God simply cannot do some things. Preventing evil is one of them. God could not have stopped the evil you and others experienced. We should not blame God for the evils described in previous pages, because God could not have stopped them.

To put it more precisely, God can't prevent evil *singlehand-edly.* Putting it precisely is important, and I'll explain why as we move through these chapters. God cannot stop evil by acting alone.

Notice I'm not saying God *won't* prevent evil. I'm saying God *can't.* The difference between "won't" and "can't" is huge.

Many people feel comfortable saying God won't stop *all* evil but does stop some. Those who say God doesn't always stop evil usually say God "allows" it. They think God freely permits the pointless pain He could singlehandedly prevent. God chooses not to intervene, they say, or decides not to interrupt evil in progress.

It makes no sense to say God allows genuine evil.

There are big problems with saying God *won't* stop evil. "Won't" and "allow" imply God *could* prevent abuse and tragedy. Saying "God allows evil" either means God doesn't care enough to intervene or the horrors are, in some mysterious way, for our good.

I can't believe either is true. I think God always cares, and genuine evil doesn't make things better overall. If preventing were possible, a loving God would prevent the horrific suffering we and others endure.

It makes no sense to say God *allows* genuine evil.

A LOVING PERSON PREVENTS PREVENTABLE EVIL

The "God allows evil" view prevails in the minds of so many. So let's explore it more. Asking this question can help: Does a loving person allow abuse, tragedy, and evil this person could prevent?

Think about that a moment.

Do we think a loving mother would freely allow an infant to drown? Do we think loving citizens allow terrorists to torture innocent children? Would you think your uncle loving if he allowed sex traffickers to kidnap your sister or wife? Do loving doctors let infants die when they could easily heal them? Do loving people allow beheadings of the innocent if stopping decapitations were possible?

No.

Perfect love prevents preventable evil.

Despite believing loving people wouldn't allow the evil they can block, many believe God allows the evil God can block. They think God permits needless suffering and avoidable horrors despite being able to stop them. They think God allows rape, torture, genocide, child abuse, and more. Someone may have even said God allowed *your* suffering!

It makes no sense to believe a perfectly loving God allows the evil this God can stop.

We know from experience, of course, sometimes we can't stop the evil we'd *like* to stop. Many things are beyond our ability. We can't entirely control others or circumstances, so we don't blame good people for failing to do what they can't do. They're not guilty.

God is different ... at least the omnipotent God most believe in.

Most believe God *could* control others entirely. They think God has the power to do anything. Some say God gives free will but could override, withdraw, or fail to give that freedom. God is sovereignly free to do anything, they claim, because God's power is unlimited.

If God can control evildoers, we should blame God for allowing the atrocities they commit. The God who fails to prevent preventable genuine evil is morally reprehensible. The God capable of control is at least partly to blame for the evils we've endured. He could have stopped them singlehandedly.

Perfect love prevents preventable evil.

The God who allows evil is guilty.

A guilty person, by definition, isn't perfectly good. Guilt and goodness stand in opposition. And we can't trust a guilty God to love consistently. In fact, a God who allows genuine evil isn't worthy of our whole-hearted love. We may fear Him, but we can't worship that God with full admiration.

We shouldn't trust a God who allows evil.

STOOD BY AND ALLOWED?

Claire sent me a Facebook message last year. In it, she talked about the sexual abuse she has endured. My heart seized in my chest as I read the details. No one should experience such awfulness!

Claire said she didn't think God abused her. She blamed family members, boyfriends, and a stranger. She also didn't believe God was punishing her. To her thinking, sexual abuse is not divine discipline.

But she had always wondered why God *allowed* it. If God is omnipotent and loving, why would He permit men to violate her body and mind? Why didn't God intervene?

According to her note, Claire found help from my book *The Uncontrolling Love of God*. It offered well-reasoned beliefs and helpful language to make sense of God's love and her pain. She was relieved to read God couldn't stop what happened. God wasn't permitting her abuse.

I'll never forget one sentence in her note: "I no longer think God stood by and allowed what happened."

The God who "won't" prevent evil could have stopped Claire's abuse. That God stood by and did not rescue. Claire cannot believe anyone who allows sexual abuse — including God — is truly loving. How could she trust an abuse-allowing God?

Claire came to believe God *cannot* prevent evil singlehandedly. An uncontrolling God works lovingly to the utmost in every situation, even when horrific things occur. But the God of uncontrolling love cannot control creatures.

To Claire, the difference between "can't" and "won't" is the difference between thinking God couldn't stop her molesters or thinking God stood by and allowed them.

WOULD JESUS STOP EVIL?

I wonder what Jesus would have done.

I do my best to follow the ways of Jesus. I try to love like he loved. So when trying to figure out what love looks like, I sometimes wonder, "What would Jesus do in this situation?" WWJD? Answering that question well and living it every day are the heart of my life as a Christian.

Christians typically say Jesus offers the clearest portrayal of God's love. "If you want to know what God is like," the saying goes, "look at Jesus." Jesus reveals God.

Let's imagine what Jesus might do if he were physically present when Claire was molested. Would he intervene? Can you imagine Jesus standing by, allowing it? Can you imagine Jesus a passive bystander to an evil he could prevent?

I can't.

I can't imagine Jesus saying, "I'm here with you, Claire. I could stop your abuse, but I'll stand by and allow it."

If Jesus could halt Claire's horrors, I think he would. He would stop any sexual abuse he could. Jesus would prevent preventable evil.

If Jesus wouldn't allow evil, neither would God.

If Jesus is our clearest revelation of God, why should we think God allows abuse? If he would act for good to the greatest extent possible, why think God does otherwise?

If Jesus wouldn't allow evil, neither would God.

If we look at suffering and abuse through the lens of Jesus' love, we will not think God can stop evil singlehandedly. God would also prevent preventable evil. We need to rethink God's power in light of the love Jesus expresses.

EVEN A POWERFUL GOD CAN'T DO SOME THINGS

Saying "God can't stop evil" makes some people uneasy. "But this is the God who created the universe!" they say. "This is the Sovereign Lord." "This is the God of the Bible: the God of miracles, resurrections, and more." "This is G-O-D!"

I understand these reactions. New ideas take time to absorb, and the idea God can't prevent evil singlehandedly is new to most. But the Bible is example number one that God encourages us to think in new ways. Personal tragedy and unnecessary suffering prompt us to seek beliefs more helpful than the ones we've been handed.

It would be a mistake to think the God I describe is inactive or a wimp. The God who can't prevent evil is our Creator. If we define divine power carefully, this God can rightly be called "almighty." The God who can't control others does miracles, healings, resurrections, and more.[3]

The God who can't prevent evil is still powerful!

God is not feeble or aloof but strong and active. We should worship the great, amazing, and mighty God of love who cannot prevent evil singlehandedly. God is the most powerful Lover in the universe. I praise this God often!

So why can't a powerful and loving God prevent evil?

My answer starts with the Bible. It surprises many to discover that biblical writers say God cannot do some things. "God cannot lie," says Titus (1:2). "God cannot be tempted," says James (1:13). "God cannot grow tired," says Isaiah (40:28).

I especially like a statement from the Apostle Paul: "When we are faithless, He remains faithful," Paul writes, "because God cannot deny himself" (2 Tim. 2:13).

"God cannot deny himself" presents us a key idea, and I'll return to it shortly. At this point, I simply want to say the *Bible* says God can't do some activities. It's biblical to say God's power is limited.

It also surprises people when they discover most leading theologians in history have said God can't do some things. They say God can't stop existing, for instance, because God exists necessarily. God can't make a rock so big that even God cannot lift it. God cannot change the past, many theologians say. God cannot sin. And so on.

The Bible says God can't do some things.

C.S. Lewis put it this way: "Not even Omnipotence can do what is self-contradictory."[4]

These statements — in the Bible and by leading theologians — assume truths about God's nature. Inspired writers and wise saints identify actions God *cannot* take and things God *cannot* do because of who God *is*.

God cannot oppose God's own nature.

GOD IS LOVE

Who we think God is makes an immense difference for what we think God does.

So ... who *is* God?

Big question! We might be tempted to say we have no idea. Who are we to know what God is like? More than a few people — from scholars to the average Jane or Joe — avoid speculating about God. Some claim only to know what God is *not*.

Fools say they know God fully. An overconfident person claims to have God figured out. As I see it, God is beyond our total knowing, and just about every theologian would agree with me. God cannot be fully comprehended.

We do have *some* ideas, intuitions, or knowledge of God, however. Nearly everyone wonders about ultimate questions and the possibility of an Ultimate Reality most people call "God." In our hearts, we have ideas about the divine, even if they are partial and imprecise. Besides, it makes sense to many that God would self-reveal, because God likely wants to be known.

We cannot know much with certainty, and we are often wrong about our views. But we *can* know God in part, though our knowledge is foggy and incomplete.

In humility, we should try to understand God better. We ought to reflect deeply on scripture, our intuitions, our experiences, and what wise people say. We ought to use our heads and our hearts.

Besides, it makes no sense to say we believe in God but say we have no idea who God is!

I rely a lot — but not exclusively — on the Bible for my knowledge of God. The Bible is not a logical system, and it says many things. We interpret the Bible through our life lens and try to make sense of it. Saying "I rely on the Bible" doesn't mean I know everything nor that the Bible tells us everything about God. But scripture has been a valuable resource for many and for me as we try to understand.

Unfortunately, some Christians use the Bible as a weapon. Victims cringe when a Bible thumper quotes a verse to "prove" why God causes or allows suffering. The Bible can be a trauma trigger, and survivors often need a break from self-described "Bible Experts." Some texts strike terror in our hearts when not understood through the lens of love.

Other Christians treat the Bible like a medicine bottle and its verses like pills. "You've got a problem?" they ask, "Here, take a scripture pill. It'll cure what ails you."

Or they treat the Bible like a magic book. Say the right words — incantations — and presto ... all questions are answered. "The Bible clearly says ..." these people begin sentences.

I don't think the Bible works like that. The broad themes of the Bible help us make sense of God and life. But we must resist thinking the Bible is a weapon, medicine bottle, or magic book. And it's not a systematic theology. While it's important to drill down to explore the details, it's more important to grasp the major ideas of the Bible.

Above all, the Bible teaches that God is loving.

Above all, the Bible teaches that God is loving. Hurting people like you and me need this message. The Old Testament bears witness to the steadfast love of God, and so does the New Testament. Jesus most clearly reveals divine love. We find profound statements about God's love throughout scripture.

Some biblical passages, I admit, describe God as unmerciful. Not every passage paints a picture of pure divine love. Bible passages that speak of God as unmerciful reflect the frustration, hurt, or anger of those suffering. They express the cries of the oppressed. Those passages don't provide an accurate description of the God who always loves. The majority of biblical passages, stories, and statements indicate God loves everyone all the time. And I accept the majority witness.

In his words, life, death, and resurrection, Jesus reveals divine love most clearly. The children's song is true: "Jesus loves me, this I know, for the Bible tells me so." In fact, Jesus' life of love inspires me to follow him.

The witness to God's love comes to a crescendo near the Bible's end. A simple phrase expresses this: "God is love" (1 Jn. 4:8, 16). Believers interpret the phrase in various ways, but "God is love" provides grounds to believe with confidence God always loves everyone. As poet Charles Wesley puts it, "Thy name and thy nature is love."

To love is to act intentionally, in response to God and others, to promote overall well-being.

And what is love? Love is purposeful action in relation to God and others that aims to do good. Love advances well-being. It fosters flourishing, abundant life, and blessedness. To put it formally, to love is to act intentionally, in response to God and others, to promote overall well-being.

God's love always works for the good, because God is love.

GOD'S NATURE IS UNCONTROLLING LOVE

To make sense of the idea that God *can't* prevent evil single-handedly, we need something more. For various reasons — including the needless pain and suffering we experience — it makes sense to think God's love is *inherently* uncontrolling.

Love does not overrule or override. It does "not force itself on others," to quote the Apostle Paul (1 Cor. 13:5). Love does not manipulate, dominate, or dictate in ways that allow no response. Love does not control.

When I say God "can't" prevent evil, I mean God is unable to control people, other creatures, or circumstances that cause evil. Because God always loves and God's love is uncontrolling, God *cannot* control. The God who can't control others or circumstances can't prevent evil singlehandedly.

God's love governs what God can do.

I can imagine the cries of some who read these statements. "Are you saying God is limited?" they wonder. "Who are you to limit God?" Despite what I've quoted from the Bible and theologians, the idea God cannot do something strikes many as heretical. "I have faith in an *unlimited* God," they respond.

It's important to recognize that *I* am not placing limits on God. Rather, God's loving *nature* determines, shapes, or governs what God can do. External powers, natural laws, or Satan do not essentially limit God. Constraints to God's power don't come from outside.

God also doesn't freely choose to be self-limited. God isn't voluntarily deciding not to control others when doing so is possible. That's the "God won't" view. Rather than externally limited or voluntarily self-limited, God's nature of love directs what God does.

God's loving nature determines, shapes, or governs what God can do.

Divine love always self-gives and others-empowers. It gives freedom to complex creatures such as you and me. It gives agency and self-organization to less complex creatures like organisms and cells. God's love is the source of both the spontaneity and regularity we see in nature and the universe. As Creator, God gives existence to all creation. All these gifts are irrevocable (Rm. 11:29).[5]

Because God's love self-gives and others-empowers, and because God loves all creatures from the most complex to the least, God cannot control. God loves everyone and everything, so God cannot control anyone or anything. This means a God of uncontrolling love cannot control evildoers to prevent their dastardly deeds.

We earlier read the passage from the Bible saying, "God cannot deny himself." We now see how this applies to questions of God's power and evil. If God's nature is love and love never controls, God would have to deny his love to control others. But God can't do that.

The limits to divine power come from God's nature of love.

I call this view "essential kenosis." The word "kenosis" comes from the Bible and has been translated as self-giving or self-emptying. Jesus' servanthood and death on the cross profoundly illustrate God's self-giving love (Phil. 2).

Loving others is who God is and what God does.

The word "essential" indicates that self-giving and others-empowering come from God's essence. Loving others is who God is and what God does. Essential kenosis says God cannot withdraw, override, or fail to provide freedom, agency, and existence to creation. God's love always empowers, never overpowers, and is inherently uncontrolling.[6] So God can't control others.

Perhaps you now understand why God *can't* prevent evil.

THE OKLAHOMA CITY BOMBING

On April 19, 1995, Timothy McVeigh and Terry Nichols used an explosive-laden truck to bomb a federal building in Oklahoma City. One hundred and sixty-eight people died; nearly seven-hundred were injured; thousands underwent therapy for the trauma the attack caused.

McVeigh was executed for being the primary terrorist. Nichols was sentenced to life in prison. But I find most interesting the fate of their friend, Michael Fortier.

Fortier was not present at the bombing. Nor did he help prepare the bomb. He was not an active participant in this horrendous act of terror.

Michael Fortier knew what McVeigh and Nichols were planning, however, but did nothing to stop it. Fortier did not alert authorities or try to prevent this act of terror some other way. He chose to be a bystander.

Fortier was arrested and charged with the crime of failing to stop the Oklahoma City bombing. He should have warned authorities, said the jury. Found guilty, Michael Fortier was sentenced to ten years in prison.

Morally mature people do not think Fortier did the right thing allowing the terrorist attack. A loving person would not have permitted this tragedy if he could have prevented it. Although Fortier did not do this dastardly deed, he failed to stop it.

He's not an example of love.

Think about it: If Michael Fortier is rightly punished for failing to prevent preventable evil, why think God failing to prevent evil — if it were possible to stop — is loving and good? If it's not loving for Fortier to allow the evil he could stop, why think it's loving for God?

Everyone thinks God is stronger than Fortier. Most think God could foresee the Oklahoma City bombing long before it occurred. If Fortier is worthy of contempt, the God who allows evil is equally worthy, perhaps more so. If Fortier is guilty for allowing the bombing, a God who could stop it singlehandedly is just as guilty.

Anyone who fails to prevent preventable evil is not consistently loving.

NOT SITTING ON A HEAVENLY THRONE

We need one more element to explain why God cannot prevent evil singlehandedly. This idea builds from the traditional belief that God is a universal spirit.

Believers have for millennia struggled to comprehend God's form or constitution. Is God located somewhere, nowhere, or everywhere? Can we see, hear, taste, smell, or touch deity? Does the Creator have a body like creatures do?

The Bible does not clearly answer these questions. The majority of texts say God does not have a localized divine body. They say God is a universal spirit present to all creation. And we cannot perceive this universal Spirit with our five senses.

Every creature is different from God in a crucial way: they have localized bodies that can exert some measure of bodily impact upon others. But God has no localized divine body.

As a kid, I remember reading comic books depicting God as a huge, faceless body. He — and it was always "He" — sat on heaven's throne and wore a white robe. Beams of light extended from all sides. I remember thinking, *God must steam-iron his robe before posing for artists!*

I was not impressed by these drawings. *How could God be present to the entire universe if sitting on a throne in the clouds?* I wondered. I also remember reading the words of the Apostle John: "No one has ever seen God" (1 Jn. 4:12). Other Bible verses speak of God being present to all creation, all at once. Early on, I doubted that God posed stiffly on a heavenly throne or lounged after hours on a celestial La-Z-Boy.

Many faith traditions insist God has no form. Some even consider drawings of God blasphemous ... comic books be damned! Physical objects become idols if we consider them literally divine. While religious icons may direct our thoughts toward God, rightly understood they are not deities.

God is a universal spirit without a localized body.

Like most theologians throughout history, I think God is a universal spirit without a localized body. Jesus put it simply: "God is spirit" (Jn. 4:24), and other biblical texts agree. Theologians often say God is "incorporeal," which means without a body, or "immaterial." Because God is a universal spirit, God doesn't have shape, height, and weight like we do.

The writers of the Bible use various words to describe the "stuff" of which God is constituted. Some compare God to breath, a mind, smoke, or the wind. None of these involve a divine body.

In recent centuries, believers have compared God to gravity, light, or oxygen. These words describe God influencing creation without having a localized physical form. While most

Christians believe God, as spirit, was specially incarnated in Jesus, they don't think God exists essentially as a localized, physical figure.

God is a bodiless, universal spirit.

A BODILESS SPIRIT

Saying God is a universal spirit plays a crucial role in explaining why God cannot prevent the evil that creatures can sometimes prevent.

To put it simply, God does not have a divine body with which to block evil or rescue creatures. By contrast, creatures *do* have bodies to exert bodily impact on others. And creatures sometimes use their bodies to stop evil.

Imagine you and I are walking along a busy street. Without looking for traffic, you step off the sidewalk onto the pavement. In doing so, you fail to notice a monster truck roaring down the street toward you. I see it and pull you from the truck's path. Startled and unnerved, you imagine what might have happened!

Notice in this imaginary scenario, you acted freely when stepping into the street. No one forced you; no one controlled you. And notice I was able to thwart your free decision by using my body (specifically my hand). I saved you from at least severe injury and perhaps death — a loving act — by stopping your body from moving in the direction you wanted.

If it's loving for me to prevent you from freely hurting yourself, wouldn't it be loving for God to do the same? If I can sometimes thwart the free actions of others, why can't God?

Or imagine you're camping with family. One evening while standing around a roaring fire, your three-year-old niece marches toward the flames — of her own free will — in a flammable nightgown. Standing nearby, you grab her by the sleeve, saving her from extensive burns. Across the fire, her father sees the whole affair and thanks you profusely.

If it's loving for you to stop your niece from freely hurting herself, wouldn't it be loving for God to do the same? If we can sometimes obstruct another person's free choices, why can't God?

Here's where "God is a universal spirit without a physical body" matters.

God has no divine hand, literally speaking, to snatch us from the path of oncoming cars or grab us before entering a fire. God has no divine arms and legs to carry people from a warzone. God has no body to stand between gunmen and potential victims. God has no arms to wrap around a distraught person to keep her from cutting herself. But because creatures have localized, physical bodies, they sometimes can prevent evil.

A bodiless, universal spirit cannot do what embodied creatures sometimes can. Despite having no body, God is present and active in all situations. Divine power is direct but persuasive, widespread but wooing, causal but uncontrolling. God's loving activity makes a difference without imposing control or using a divine body.

God is a universal spirit and has no localized divine body to stop evil.

God calls creatures to use their bodies for good. When I pull you from the path of a truck or you save your niece from the flames, God was the loving inspiration for this good. When we respond appropriately to God, we might say we become God's body. This isn't literally true, of course. Cooperative creatures extend God's activity. But they aren't literally divine. We become God's representational hands and feet.

Embodied creatures can also refuse to cooperate with God. Victims know this better than most. Humans and other creatures can refuse to act as God's hands and feet. We rightly blame uncooperative creatures for causing or allowing evils God did not want.

God is a universal spirit and has no localized divine body to stop evil.

WE'RE NOT ROBOTS

As a loving Creator, God creates uncontrollable creatures.

By "uncontrollable creatures," I mean God constantly gives freedom, self-organization, agency, or the power to act, depending on a creature's complexity. God creates all things, continually influences everything, but controls nothing.

To put it another way, God doesn't create robots.

God creates free creatures, and humans seem to be the freest of all. No one is entirely free, of course. Our histories, bodies, environments, genes, and other factors constrain and shape us. Other people and factors expand or decrease our freedom. Unlimited freedom is a myth.

We can be influenced by others even when we don't want to be. Sometimes this uninvited influence helps. Infants benefit from the motherly love they do not freely choose, for instance. Firefighters sometimes carry unconscious victims from burning houses. We benefit from the loving sacrifices of ancestors we've never met.

But uninvited influence sometimes harms. Assault survivors know this. So do those who suffer from other forms of abuse. The sins of our fathers and mothers or strangers — both in the past and present — harm us in ways we often cannot avoid. Victims know unwanted violence damages and destroys.

We live amid relationships that help or harm.

The idea that a loving God does not create robots helps us make sense of God's acting. Bible stories tell of God influencing humans, donkeys, trees, heavens, and more. Sometimes God's action is dramatic. But God's action is mostly subtle and understated.

It's tempting to think the Bible says God *alone* made something happen, but the Bible never explicitly says this. Some think God takes over a creature's body or controls it for some purpose, but the Bible doesn't explicitly say this either. If it were true, God would temporarily make that person a robot. Automatons are predetermined machines not capable of real relationships nor able to love freely.

An uncontrolling God neither creates us as robots nor temporarily roboticizes us. From God's special incarnation in Jesus to activity in the smallest creatures, God acts without controlling. And this lack of control — at all levels of existence — makes loving relationships possible.

> The Bible never explicitly says God alone made something happen.

When complex creatures cooperate with God, good things happen. Love flourishes. Peace blossoms. Astonishing miracles can occur. When complex creatures fail to cooperate with God, evil happens. Unnecessary pain and pointless suffering occur. The demons dance.

Because a loving God did not make us and others robots, good and bad are possible.

GOD BATTLED, GOD LOST

Four-year-old Henry developed a brain tumor. In her book, *Lord Willing*? Henry's mother, Jessica, describes how she tried to cope.

Friends and strangers offered typical explanations. Some said God gave Henry the tumor because it pleased Him to do so! "Am I truly to believe that God is so limited in creativity and resources," Jessica says in response, "that he *had* to slay my four-year-old son to bring about good?"

To those who think Henry's pain and death were God's punishment, Jessica asks rhetorically powerful questions: "Should we conclude that *all* suffering is God's discipline? What about nations of starving people? Or millions dying in the Holocaust? What about when little boys die from big tumors, in their parents' beds? Could this ever, ever be called love?"

Jessica's explanation for her son's death makes more sense. "Henry wasn't healed on Earth," she says, "but not because a divine blueprint called for his death. I believe God did everything possible to maximize good and minimize evil as a vicious disease thwarted His loving will."

"I believe God battled, and I believe God lost."

If God did everything possible to help, why did Henry suffer from this tumor and eventually die? "I believe God battled, and I believe God lost," says Jessica. "For whatever reason, in that particular instance, he could not heal my little boy."

God *could not* heal her son; Jessica believes God can't prevent evil singlehandedly.

"It may sound shocking or off-putting to assert that God *can't* do something," Jessica admits. "But consider this: if God *could* prevent a rape, stop a bullet, or heal a malignant tumor, but *won't*, he's failing to demonstrate love.... And if we know anything about God, it's that he *is love*."[7]

Jessica understands the logic of uncontrolling love.

THE SHACK *ALMOST* GETS IT RIGHT

Paul Young's best-selling book, *The Shack*, tackles questions about God, love, and evil. Young is an excellent storyteller, and he weaves positive themes to offer helpful answers.[8]

The plot of Young's fictional story revolves around the abduction and murder of young Missy. The dreadful event devastates the family, especially her father Mac. He cannot understand why a loving and powerful God would allow this evil.

One day, Mac receives a mysterious letter with an invitation to the shack where police found his daughter dead. He accepts the invitation and returns to the scene only to find no one. In despair, he nearly commits suicide.

Upon leaving the shack, Mac encounters a young man who invites him to meet God. Mac accepts and spends several days talking with God, portrayed as a Trinity of three people. He also meets Wisdom personified.

The majority of the story depicts Mac in conversations with God and those who have died. Many of his questions are answered, and Mac begins to transform.

I like *The Shack*. It portrays God as warm, personable and loving rather than stern, wrathful, and aloof. When the Trinity is present, we find joy, laughter, dancing, understanding, and openness.

The Shack asks hard questions, and the answers it offers are mostly helpful. God is not portrayed as evil's cause, for instance. "I work incredible good out of unspeakable tragedies," says God. "But that doesn't mean I orchestrate them." God is present with those who suffer: "I'm in the middle of everything, working for your good." In response to Mac's anger over Missy's death, God as Trinity says, "We would like to heal it, if you would let us." And when Mac says, "Everyone knows you punish the people who disappoint you," God corrects him: "No. I don't need to punish. Sin is its own punishment."

The Shack doesn't answer a question, however, those who suffer often ask: "Why didn't God *prevent* the evil I endured?"

Mac asks God, "What good comes from being murdered by a sick monster? Why don't you stop evil?" He gets no answer.

"God may not do evil," says Mac, "but He didn't stop the evil. How can Papa allow Missy's death?" Again, no answer.

The Shack doesn't answer this question: "Why doesn't God prevent evil?"

"You're the almighty God with limitless power," Mac says. "But you let my little girl die. You abandoned her." God ignores "let my little girl die" and replies to the charge of abandoning, "I was always with her."

Mac asks the right question but receives no answer. Despite the positive aspects of *The Shack*, the story offers no believable reason why a good and powerful God fails to *prevent* genuine evil.

The Shack fails to answer the primary question victims ask.

THE PROBLEM WITH MYSTERY

Several times in *The Shack*, God says to Mac, "You misunder-stand the mystery." At one point, the Spirit says, "You're trying to make sense of the world looking at an incomplete picture." Wisdom questions Mac's ability to judge good and evil, implying that he's not competent to make such judgments.

People who think God *could* stop evil often make such appeals to mystery. They rightly say God is smarter than we are. But they mistakenly think our lack of knowledge is the best answer.

When it comes to knowing God, we only know in part, so some ignorance is unavoidable. Our views of God are never 100% true. We see as if looking through a distorted windowpane.

But appealing to mystery on whether we can judge good and evil undercuts belief in God's love!

Let me explain. The major idea of *The Shack* is that we should accept, deep down, that God loves us. I endorse this idea, and it's a central theme of this book. In fact, believing God loves us, others, and all creation is the most important idea of our lives!

In *The Shack*, God scolds Mac for thinking he can judge good and evil. Mac reasons from an incomplete picture, he's told, so he *can't* know what is ultimately loving. But it's disin-genuous for God to encourage Mac to believe in love and then question Mac's ability to know what love is. That kind of mys-tery makes no sense.

If we cannot know what is good, it makes no sense to say God is good. If we don't know the difference between love and evil, we should feel no joy in thinking God loves us. After all, this love may be evil!

> *We should be wary of the God whose love is mystery, because we never know whom the Devil he may be!*

We should be wary of the God whose love is mystery, because we never know whom the Devil he may be!

If *The Shack* had said God could not prevent evil singlehandedly, it could have avoided the mystery card. And it could have answered the central question survivors ask. Accepting that God's nature is uncontrolling love makes a huge difference!

A LOVING PAPA

The Shack's greatest strength may be the picture it paints of an intimately loving God. The book's characters call God "Papa," even though God the Father is depicted as a Black woman and the Spirit is an Asian woman. Papa often talks about being "especially fond" of people. I like that!

Depicting God as a loving parent helps us understand God's persuasive influence as uncontrolling love. Of course, human parents aren't consistently loving, and some rarely love at all! God is different.

Some people mistakenly think if God doesn't control us or creation, God must not do anything. To them, God's action is either all determining or nonexistent. In this way of thinking, God either rules all or influences none.

But there's a middle way between control and absence, and that's the way of love.

Caring parents — Papas — express loving influence that neither overrules nor withdraws. Loving mothers and fathers don't micromanage or rule with an iron fist. They aren't absent or MIA either. Loving fathers and mothers guide, instruct, persuade, call, correct, convince, encourage, nudge, teach, warn, and more. None of those activities involve control.

Perhaps the best word to describe ongoing parental love is "nurture." Nurturing involves cultivating the lives of children by providing positive experiences, wise instruction, and forgiveness. But nurturing implies working alongside the agencies of others, not controlling them.

Parents who love consistently imitate God's steadfast love. In fact, Jesus called God "Abba," a word for an intimately and consistently loving Father. Abba is Papa.

Children wisely cooperate with parental love. This cooperation assumes free obedience to positive influence. When children cooperate with love, the results are beautiful, meaningful, and constructive. Wise children of God follow Papa's loving lead.

Children foolishly rebel against loving parents. When anyone rebels against love, the result is pointless pain, unnecessary suffering, and genuine evil. Resisting love leads to destruction.

God acts like a loving parent who nurtures children.

A WOOING SUITOR

The courting beau offers another example of uncontrolling love. In courtship, partners act in ways that lure, entice, or invite without controlling, manipulating, or dictating. Their loving action is influential without overpowering.

Just as some parents are poor examples of love, some romantic partners fail to love well. But an amorous relationship of mutual love is good for everyone. Giving-and-receiving love promotes well-being.

The typical marriage proposal highlights this active but un-controlling love. When I asked my wife to marry me, I acted to invite her response. For my wish to become a reality, she had to consent. She had to choose to say, "Yes!"

The successful marriage proposal requires an accepting response.

God acts like a loving suitor. Nothing can stop God from inviting us, moment-by-moment, to a loving relationship. God's uncontrolling love is uncontrolla-ble! But we can choose not to co-operate. We can fail to say, "Yes!" When we do not respond appropri-ately, the mutual relationship of love God desired is thwarted. God's will is not done on Earth as it is in heaven. But "Yes" leads to abundant life!

God's uncontrolling love is uncontrollable!

Even a successful proposal does not a successful marriage make. The initial "Yes!" doesn't guarantee "happily ever after." The free cooperation must continue in the marriage. If one tries to control the other, the relationship becomes unhealthy. Love cannot be forced. This is true in marriage and true in our relationship with God.

God acts like a wooing suitor asking for a partner's hand and a spouse pursuing a lifetime of mutual love.

BRAVE

Early in life, my friend Janyne endured sexual abuse. She sup-pressed this trauma for years, but it eventually surfaced in de-structive ways. At one point, she nearly threw herself off a cliff!

In her book, *Brave: A Personal Story of Healing Childhood Trauma*, Janyne describes how she and her counselor worked toward healing. The process was intense and prolonged. It involved coming to terms with childhood memories and comprehending how abuse affected her thinking and living.

A major part of recovery came as she changed her view of God. "The day I realized I had choices was the day I understood God was not controlling," writes Janyne. "He did not control me on the cliff; I chose to turn and live. But so did all those who hurt me. We all had free will. And I don't need to say nonsensical things such as, 'God allowed my abuse to build my character.'"[9]

Janyne rejected the idea that God had a predetermined plan that included abuse. She came to believe God was always involved, calling her to decisions in light of positive or negative circumstances. God is a loving guide not a coercive manipulator. And not even God could control Janyne's abuser.

"Outside of an understanding of an uncontrolling God," Janyne writes, "there is no potential for truly transcending the human experience of trauma, living life abundantly, and worshipping freely. The God who controls could not be my anchor. But the God who loves me, comforts me, brings me support by prompting the good actions of others, and guides my choices most certainly can!"

"The God who controls could not be my anchor."

Janyne found comfort believing God could not have stopped her abuse alone. A loving God who *could* have stopped it *should* have.

BELIEF # 1 — GOD CAN'T PREVENT EVIL SINGLEHANDEDLY

To make sense of life, we should believe God can't prevent evil singlehandedly.

Saying God can't stop evil helps survivors overcome thinking God was mad or punishing them. Victims don't have to think God stood by and allowed their harm. They don't need to worry God could have stopped their tragedy or abuse.

God can't.

Family and friends of survivors may also find it helpful to believe God can't prevent evil singlehandedly. They no longer need to think evil is part of some master plan. They don't need to wonder why a loving God would allow pointless pain and unnecessary suffering. They no longer need to recite the tired and untrue rationalizations why God does not stop suffering.

Of course, most people need time to process the "God can't" idea. You may be one of them. The idea is new and easily misunderstood, so I'll return to it throughout this book. We need time to digest radical ideas.

No single idea is sufficient for solving the problem of evil. But the idea God can't prevent evil singlehandedly is indispensable. We must believe it to make good sense of our lives and existence in general.

Thinking God can't prevent evil singlehandedly clears obstacles to believing in God, understanding love, and moving toward healing.

Questions

1. Why might some people be shocked to hear God can't prevent evil singlehandedly?

2. What problems arise when someone says God "allows" evil?

3. Why does it matter that we believe God's nature is uncontrolling love?

4. If you've read *The Shack* or seen the movie, what did you like or not like?

5. Why is it important to believe God doesn't create us as robots or temporarily roboticize us?

6. Why should we believe God is a bodiless spirit who can't prevent evil that creatures like us sometimes can?

7. What is helpful about the idea that God acts like a loving parent or suitor who needs cooperation? And how can this help us evaluate our family or romantic relationships?

For resources that address God's power in helpful ways, see
GodCant.com

ENDNOTES

A SOLUTION TO EVIL

1. Russell Moore, "Where is God in a Mass Shooting? https://www.russellmoore.com/2017/10/02/god-mass-shooting/ Accessed 6/21/2018.

2. Those who want to explore the details of this book's proposals might read my scholarly writings, such as The Uncontrolling Love of God (IVP Academic), The Nature of Love (Chalice), or Defining Love (Brazos). I also recommend Uncontrolling Love (SacraSage), a book of accessible essays written by 80 wise people.

1. GOD CAN'T PREVENT EVIL

3. I define power carefully and show how an uncontrolling love can do miracles in my book, The Uncontrolling Love of God. See especially chapters 7 and 8.

4. C. S. Lewis, Miracles: A Preliminary Study (New York: HarperCollins, 2001), 90.

5. I spell out these issues in detail in The Uncontrolling Love of God: An Open and Relational Account of Providence (Downers Grove, Ill.: Intervarsity Academic, 2015).

6. For more, see The Uncontrolling Love of God, ch. 7.

7. Jessica Kelley, Lord Willing? Wrestling with God's Role in Child's Death (Harrisonburg, VA: Herald, 2016),

8. Wm. Paul Young, The Shack (Windblown, 2008).

9. Janyne McConnaughey, Brave: A Personal Story of Healing Childhood Trauma (Greeley, Colo.: Cladach, 2018), 207.

For the remainder of this book, visit your favorite bookseller...

Best Seller

GOD CAN'T

HOW TO BELIEVE IN GOD
AND LOVE
AFTER TRAGEDY,
ABUSE, AND OTHER EVILS

THOMAS JAY OORD

Author of the Award-Winning Book, *The Uncontrolling Love of God*

Questions and Answers

for

God Can't

Table of Contents

Preface

I wrote this book to offer answers.

God Can't readers sent me great questions after finishing the book. Most found the book's arguments persuasive. Some readers said the ideas transformed their lives.[1]

For many readers, the book raised additional questions about God, the world, and their personal beliefs. Some questions were theological in orientation. Some were practical and others personal. Nearly every question seemed to have emerged from careful deliberation about the implications of God's uncontrolling love.

Answering each question well would require full-length books. I don't have time to write that many books and you don't have time to read them. I'm providing chapter-length responses here. I apologize for not answering *every* good question I am asked. Drop me an email or a note on social media if you want to ask something I did not address here.

My tone in this book is conversational. At times, my answers may sound academic, but I try to avoid technical language. I intend to be accessible and understandable. I use a tone typical of a podcast interview or popular lecture.

I hope this book becomes a valuable resource in your ongoing quest to love God, others, all creation, and yourself. As I see it, love isn't limited to matters of the heart. It involves the most profound elements of our intellect. In the quest for wisdom, love integrates reason with the widest array of experiences. Answering our questions well can help us love with confidence.

I'm interested to see the response to this book. I don't pretend it offers the last word on every subject. There will always be more to ponder. I don't expect everyone who embraces the uncontrolling love perspective to agree with what I say in this book. But I think these ideas can help you and me explore the implications and applications of God's uncontrolling love.

Thomas Jay Oord

INTRODUCTION

God Can't is Helping People

I wasn't prepared for the impact of God Can't: How to Believe in God and Love after Tragedy, Abuse, and Other Evils. Reader responses blew me away!

Several friends urged me to take the idea of God's uncontrolling love and make it accessible to a wider audience. They believed many more would find this view of God fruitful. I was willing to act on their encouragement, because I wanted to expand and add new ideas. *God Can't* was born.

I'm happy to say the book has been an Amazon best-seller in multiple categories. I'm even happier that the ideas in it are helping people. Readers frequently send notes thanking me for introducing them to the uncontrolling love of God perspective. For some, the ideas have been life changing! Others write to say the book helped them connect intellectual dots previously disconnected.

Given the response, it seemed appropriate to begin this book with a brief look at the readers of *God Can't*.

READERS OF *GOD CAN'T*

Most responses to *God Can't* come through email or social media. A few are hand-written and given in person or sent through postal service. Some take me out for coffee to pose questions. And scholars query me, seeking clarity as they explore this fresh perspective.

I want to share a few responses. I've focused on those that offer a taste of the impact *God Can't* is having. All names have been changed to protect the authors.

One of the first notes addressed God and sexual abuse. The writer found helpful the idea God can't stop evil singlehandedly. It would be the first of *many* similar notes...

> Let me tell you a bit about my story. I'm a survivor of sexual abuse, a lot and for a long time by my brother. In the midst of the worst years of my life, I had a very vivid dream of God walking over to my bed as I was being raped. God simply reached out, held my hand, and cried.
>
> For a few short days, I was elated: God hadn't left me after all! Then came the anger. Anger that God was there, and instead of stopping it, God simply held my hand and watched!
>
> For a long time, years, I was angry about that. I prayed for a breakthrough. But I never got it, so I buried it. Now paging, praying, and contemplating through your book, I can see more clearly what may have been happening. God could not stop my brother; God gives free will. How could God have stopped him?

*The reality is God couldn't, not that God didn't. For
me, this is a complete game-changer.*

—Monica

Another note addressed how *God Can't* helped the reader
think about divine action and childhood cancer. This man told
me about his son...

*My three-year-old son died from a particularly difficult
form of childhood cancer. I can no longer believe the notion that "God is in control." What loving parent would
choose to stand by while their child walked into traffic...
if that parent could stop the child? I know of none.*

*When it comes to God, there has to be more than
God choosing to allow evil to happen.*

—Geoffrey

Many notes addressed the importance of saying God *can't*
rather than God *won't*. So many survivors have been told God
sometimes chooses to allow evil, which leaves them with painful question. Here's one of those notes...

*I've always heard people speak of allowing something.
But it never sits well with my soul. If God allows one
thing, where do we stop with how much He does allow
good or bad? If God can control, where do we stop with
that idea?*

*I've never been able to accept God controls or even
allows, because that would mean God allowed my*

childhood torture. God did not exercise control to stop it. Unacceptable!

This bad view of God has led me to drift in and out of a crisis of faith. I thought God was controlling or allowing the harm I endured. I had no other way to conceptualize it. And I was told it's not okay to ask hard questions.

The idea God can't stop evil singlehandedly articulates what I had intuited but had not yet expressed.

—Cami

A pastor sent a note saying *God Can't* helped him think differently about suffering. The note mirrored several sent by caregivers and spiritual counselors...

As a pastor, I've heard people offer a myriad of ways to make sense of tragedy. Many attribute tragedy to the will of God. They focus on the mystery of God's ways as their way of managing more troubling thoughts about God's choice to harm or allow harm.

While I would not presume to tell a survivor how to make peace with God, many would benefit from the opportunity to consider the "God Can't" option. In it, God neither sent them harm nor stood by and allowed it to take place when God could have done otherwise.

—Jim

A young woman sent me this letter after an event at which I spoke. It represents many letters from survivors and victims who found *God Can't* helpful...

If God could, why would God allow two teenage boys to tie me up to a tree at age eight to be tortured and molested? Then I was told I was defiled, and God couldn't love me anymore.

Why would this God allow that same child to endure an attempted abduction at age 12? Then allow her to be stalked and raped by a man in her church?

I just can't see a God who allows children to go through all of this. I can't see God allowing a woman to be taken into sex slavery, for instance, or allow children to die from horrific diseases.

After reading just part of your book, I can see the God who "allows" these things is not a God of total love.

—Angie

Finally, another note from a pastor:

I finished your book last night, and I just can't stop thinking about it. Thank you for this amazing book! It's a mind-blowing, game-changing book about God's uncontrolling love.

As a cancer survivor and someone who struggles with chemo-induced pulmonary fibrosis, I've tried to make sense of why God allows illnesses. I've struggled with why God heals some people and doesn't heal others. Or why God allows evil and abuse. And so on.

This book provides the first explanation that I've resonated with. I highly recommend it to those who have faced tragedy, abuse, and other evils!

—Pablo

These excerpts are just the tip of the iceberg. *God Can't* is making a powerful impact. As I write this follow-up book, it's been about a year since *God Can't* was published. I fully expect the ideas to help many more people![1]

SUMMING UP

To set the stage for this book, *Questions and Answers for God Can't*, let me briefly review key ideas in *God Can't*. This review will help me as I answer questions in the upcoming chapters.

Let me recap.

God Can't uses true stories to explain why we need a view of God different from what most of us have learned. The book rejects the typical answers to why a good, loving, and powerful God would not prevent evil.

The problem of evil is the primary reason most atheists say they can't believe in God. And I suspect God's relation to evil and suffering is the number one question asked by those who do believe in God.

I often say in *God Can't* that God loves everyone and everything. I define "love" as acting intentionally, in relational response to God and others, to promote overall well-being. This definition applies to the love both creatures and God express. Those who imagine they've solved the problem of evil by saying God's love is entirely different from ours haven't solved the problem at all. Such love is utterly incomprehensible, and such absolute mysteries don't bring us closer to making sense of life.

I also believe genuinely evil events occur. A genuinely evil occurrence makes the world, all things considered, worse than it might have been. Evil events do not make our lives better overall.

Some people reject the idea of evil. But we all act as if we think genuine evils occur. We all act as if some things make the world worse than it might have been. Besides, it's hard to look at horrific events and say they're not genuinely evil. The Christian tradition assumes some events make the world worse, and it calls at least some of them sinful.

God Can't Prevent Evil

The first and probably most controversial point of the book comes in Chapter One: *God can't singlehandedly prevent evil.* It's important to distinguish between saying God *can't* prevent evil and God *won't* prevent evil. Many people will say God won't always prevent evil. They're uncomfortable saying God can't singlehandedly stop it.

A loving person prevents the evil that person is capable of preventing. To think a loving God stands by and allows genuine evil runs counter to what love is really like. It runs counter to the love Jesus expressed. Saying "love allows evil" makes no sense.

I'm not the first theologian to say God can't do some things. The majority say God can't do what is illogical. God can't make 2 + 2 = 387. God can't make a married bachelor. And so on.

Many theologians also say God cannot contradict God's own nature. If it's God's nature to exist, God must exist. If it's God's nature to love, God must love. God simply can't act in an evil way or cease to exist.

Biblical writers sometimes mention actions God cannot take. My favorite example comes from the Apostle Paul's letter to Timothy. "When we are faithless," writes Paul, "God remains faithful, because God *cannot* deny himself" (2 Tim. 2:13).

My purpose in saying that God must do some things and can't do others says God's love is inherently uncontrolling.

Divine love is self-giving and others-empowering. Because God necessarily loves everyone and everything, God must self-give and others-empower. This means God can't control anyone or anything. Uncontrolling love comes first in God's nature.

Saying God can't make round squares, can't stop existing, or can't control others leads us to wonder if God is limited. The uncontrolling love view seems to describe a God with limited powers, at least compared to how most people think of God.

Most people have an incoherent view of God. They say or think God can do things inherently impossible for loving beings to do. Incoherent theology does not appeal to thinking people.

In chapter one, I also explore an idea most Christians, Jews, and Muslims affirm: that God does not have a localized body like we do. Instead, God is an omnipresent bodiless spirit. God is incorporeal, to use the classic language.

Saying God is bodiless helps us understand why we sometimes can use our bodies to thwart evil, but God can't thwart them. We can sometimes grab someone from falling into a pit, for instance. But God doesn't have a divine hand to grab falling people.

All good ultimately stems from God, because God is the source of good. When we use our arms to rescue people from pits, we can say God inspired our bodily actions. We act as God's metaphorical hands and feet. This doesn't mean we're literally gods or literally divine. But when we respond to the Spirit and do something loving, we can believe God was the inspirational source of our actions.

I also briefly address the role of mystery in the first chapter of *God Can't*. Many believers play the mystery card when the questions of God and evil emerge. "God's ways are not our ways," they say. Or "We don't understand why a loving God doesn't stop evil."

I don't play this mystery card, meaning I don't appeal to mystery rather than rethinking my view of God. I don't think I know God completely. And what I think I know about God, I don't know with absolute certainty. In that sense, even I have a role for mystery. But that role is different from playing the mystery card instead of rethinking our fundamental ideas about God. That's an idea we'll return to in future chapters.

Some who see the title, *God Can't* wonder if I'll be describing a God who watches from a distance. Or a God who does nothing at all. But the God I describe is active throughout all existence, and we all rely upon God's moment-by-moment activity.

God Feels Our Pain

The second big idea in *God Can't* says that *God feels pain*. God empathizes with those who suffer. "The Golden Rule" says we should do to others, as we would have them do to us. What I call "The Crimson Rule" says we should feel with others, as we would have them feel with us.

God is the fellow sufferer who understands. God is moved with compassion and affected by the ups and downs of our lives. God empathizes with us better than any friend could. We see this empathy most clearly in the person of Jesus of Nazareth.

Most Christian theologians have said God does not suffer. Most say God is impassable or non-relational. But the God I see described in Scripture, in Jesus, and active in the world not only influences us but is also influenced by us. God engages in giving and receiving relationships.

To solve the problem of evil, it's not enough to say God suffers with us. Some contemporary theologians affirm the idea God empathizes, but they offer, "God suffers with us" as their only answer to the problem of evil.

It's important to believe God suffers with us, but we should also believe God can't prevent evil singlehandedly. Without both ideas (and others in *God Can't*), we can't offer a believable explanation for unnecessary suffering, tragedy, abuse, and other evils.

I close Chapter Two of *God Can't* by listing ways we might feel God's love. I mention six such ways. One involves the ministry of human presence. For this, I recommend therapy and counseling. The second way is through communities of care. I readily acknowledge some faith communities don't love and care, so I recommend searching for those that do. The third way we might feel God's love is through practices like meditation, mindfulness, and prayer. Some of these activities are classic and well known; others may be new to you. Fourth, we sometimes feel God's presence in nature. I often hike in parts of the world that inspire me. The fifth way we sometimes experience God's love is through art, music, and movies. Finally, the sixth is our love for or from children, a powerful means to feel God's loving presence.

God Works to Heal

The third big idea in *God Can't* offers a framework of ideas to understand healing. God works to heal, but healing does not always occur. To reconstruct our views of healing, I offer four general beliefs.

First, *God is always present to all aspects of creation*. God never intervenes, as if coming from the outside. As one present to all creation, God always works to heal to the greatest extent possible, given the circumstances. God is the source for *all* healing that occurs.

Second, *God works alongside people, their bodies, aspects of creation, and other entities.* God works with healthcare professionals, nurses, pharmacists, medical specialists, nutritionists, and so on. God works alongside people with unique healing gifts, communities of faith, and commonsense folk wise in the ways of living. God also works alongside cells, organs, blood, muscles, and other body entities.

Third, although God always works to heal, *God can't heal singlehandedly.* God's healing work is always uncontrolling, because God always loves and never controls. Creation must cooperate. This does not mean those not healed did not have enough faith. People often have plenty of cooperative faith and work with the Great Physician. But their bodies or other factors are not conducive to God's healing work. Circumstances in our bodies and beyond them present both opportunities and challenges. Because God can't overpower or bypass agents and entities, God can't singlehandedly heal. Healing comes when creatures or entities cooperate or when the inanimate conditions of creation are conducive to healing.

Fourth, *some healing must wait until the afterlife.* I believe in continued subjective experience beyond bodily death. While there is much speculation in Scripture and among serious thinkers about what happens in the afterlife, I argue that our personal experience continues without our present bodies.

God Squeezes Good from Bad

The fourth big idea says we don't have to think God wants evil for good to emerge. We can believe God always works for good despite pain, torture, and traumas. God works with us, our bodies, smaller entities, and the larger society to squeeze whatever good can be squeezed from the bad God didn't want in the first place.

We don't have to believe everything happens for a reason. We don't have to believe God allows suffering to improve our character. We don't have to think God sends pain to punish us or teach us a lesson. Instead, we should believe God works to wring a measure of wellness from the wrong God didn't want.

God is not an outside force predetermining the course of our lives. God moves through time with us and the future is yet to be decided. When rotten things happen, God doesn't give up on the situation. God works with us and other agents, possibilities, circumstances, and data to bring whatever good can be brought from bad.

God doesn't punish. But there are natural negative consequences that come from sin and evil. Sometimes those who experience negative consequences are not the ones who failed to love. In an interrelated universe, the harmful actions of one can hurt others more than the harming actor. Evildoers and the unrighteous sometimes seem to be better off, at least in the short term.

When our suffering produces character, helps us learn a lesson, or provides wisdom, we don't have to believe God caused or allowed it to bring about good. Instead, we can say God worked to squeeze something good out of the evil God didn't want in the first place.

God Needs Our Cooperation

The final idea in *God Can't* says God needs cooperation for love to win. Instead of believing God can singlehandedly establish the ways of love, we should believe in what I call "indispensable love synergy." This synergy says God calls and empowers our responses of love.

Conventional theologians say God doesn't need us. The conventional God is like the preschool teacher who tells her kids to clean up a playroom and says they won't go home unless the room is clean. But when the children don't cooperate, she does the job herself. Traditional theologies portray God as condescending to ask us to participate in what God can do without our help. They imply our lives don't ultimately matter.

By contrast, the God of uncontrolling love needs us. Our choices, our lives, our decisions are ultimately important. God does not need us for God to exist; God will exist no matter what happens. God's needs are the needs of love. If love is relational and the results for which love aims rely upon our responses, God's needs are based on love.

We need not fear the God of uncontrolling love. God never harms us or others. We should work with God to protect ourselves and others, as God calls us to protect the weak, vulnerable, and defenseless.

Near the end of chapter five, I offer what I call the "relentless love" view of the afterlife. It says that God never gives up inviting us to relationship in this life and the next. We can always say no to love. But God never gives up inviting us to abundant life. I'll spend an entire chapter in the present book exploring the afterlife in more detail.

In sum, the five key ideas of *God Can't* provide an actual solution for why a loving and powerful God does not prevent genuine evil. These ideas, taken together, present a loving God whom we can trust without reservation.

GOD'S NATURE OF LOVE

Many readers of *God Can't* ask questions that directly or indirectly deal with my view of God's uncontrolling love. In my more academic book, *The Uncontrolling Love of God: An Open and Relational Account of Providence*, I call this view "essential kenosis." It wrestles with how we might best understand God's nature of love.[2]

Even some professional theologians avoid speculating about God's nature. Some say we should only talk about how God acts in the world. But I think it's natural to wonder who God is when we see actions we think are God-inspired.

The Bible can help us ponder God's nature. The revelation of God we find in Jesus is particularly illuminating. When we speculate about God's nature, we draw wisdom from the Christian tradition, contemporary experiences, sages and saints, science, the humanities, our own reasoning abilities, and more.

Our vision of God's nature will always be partly obscured and ambiguous. And we should be humble and tentative. But we have good reasons to believe we can make progress in understanding God, even if we can't be certain.

I believe love comes logically first in God's nature. By "first," I don't mean God's attributes line up like dominoes, and love is the first in line. I mean we should think about God's other attributes in light of love. Love should come first conceptually as we think about God.

God has other attributes, and they're important. But when our views of those attributes clash with love, we need to reformulate them in ways that harmonize with love.

When some hear me place conceptual priority on love, they'll say, "Why not make God's attributes equal, so none has priority?" Some theologians have tried to do this. But if we examine their theologies, we find they (at least implicitly) privilege some divine attributes over others.

For instance, some theologians say God's love and power are equal. But then they'll claim God has the power not to love. Or they'll say God could decide to stop loving someone. These claims reveal such theologians actually think God's power of choice comes logically prior to love. By contrast, I think love comes logically before power.

I'm not the first theologian to say love comes first in God's nature, although this view is in the minority. Nor am I the first to say God must love, although this strikes many people as unusual. I don't know anyone else, however, who adds the particular content I do when saying love comes first in God's nature. It's this content I call "essential kenosis" or "uncontrolling love" theology.

We interpret the Bible well when we use essential kenosis as our interpretive lens. This view says God cannot override, withdraw, or fail to provide the power of freedom, agency, or existence to creaturely others. Consequently, God can't control creatures or creation.

Most kenosis theologians think God voluntarily chooses to self-give power and freedom to creation. Most say God self-limits voluntarily and decides to allow space for creatures to act freely. Jürgen Moltmann is a good representative of this view of divine kenosis as voluntarily self-limiting. But the God who voluntarily self-limits could choose to un-self-limit at any time. In theologies like Moltmann's, sovereign choice to self-limit comes first in God's nature.[3] So victims and survivors wonder why God didn't un-self-limit to rescue them singlehandedly!

By contrast, essential kenosis says God is involuntarily self-limited.[4] God is self-limited in the sense that no outside force, power, or authority limits God. God's loving nature limits God's action. Consequently, God can't control others. The God who cannot control others cannot prevent evil singlehandedly.

JOHN WESLEY SAYS GOD CAN'T

I conclude this chapter by looking briefly at words from John Wesley, one of my theological heroes. It surprises even some Wesleyan scholars that Wesley claimed God could not do some things. In his sermon "On Providence," he wrestles with how to say God acts. He writes:

> *"Were human liberty taken away, men would be as incapable of virtue as stones. Therefore (with reverence be it spoken), the Almighty himself cannot do this thing. God cannot thus contradict himself or undo what he has done."*

Notice Wesley says God *cannot* do these things. He doesn't say God *chooses* not to do them. Some activities are simply not possible for an almighty God.

Wesley makes three claims in this quote. First, he says (as I do) God can't take away freedom. Secondly, he says (as I do) God can't contradict himself. And third, Wesley claims (as I do) God can't undo what has been done.

Many Christian theologians accept that God can't take away freedom. They may say God can't undermine the freedom God gives. I make the stronger argument that God *must* give freedom to complex creatures, because God's loving nature requires it. And I argue God necessarily gives agency and self-organization to smaller creatures and entities. These gifts of love are why God can't withdraw, override, or fail to give freedom, agency, or self-organization to creatures and creation.[5]

The second idea in Wesley's quote says God can't contradict God's own nature. This fits nicely with my essential kenosis theology. We might say God can't decide not to be God. This idea is central to Christian theologians who say God's essence comes prior to God's will. We'll look at this more in later chapters.

The third idea in Wesley's quote refers to God's inability to change what has already occurred. What's done is done; reverse causation is a myth. God works to *redeem* the past, but that's not the same as changing it. Wesley seems to make a claim about God's relation to time. Although he was not an open theist in the contemporary sense of that label, he endorses a view about God's relation to time that open theists like me appreciate. I suspect that if Wesley were living today, he'd identify as open and relational.

I mention John Wesley not to indicate that I'm merely presenting ideas he previously offered. There are similarities. But I'm making some bolder moves than Wesley made. While I'm not the first theologian to say God can't, my contributions explain how a particular view of God's nature resolves the problem of evil.

CONCLUSION

In this book, I'm widening the conversation. I will show how the uncontrolling love view resolves perplexing questions and concerns. Readers will probably be surprised at how my answers are both radical and yet compatible with beliefs held by everyday people.

The advantages of saying God can't do some activities because divine love is uncontrolling are wide ranging. I've addressed some in *God Can't* and *The Uncontrolling Love of God*. Other writers explore the view's benefits in a book called *Uncontrolling Love: Essays Exploring the Love of God with Introductions by Thomas Jay Oord*.[6]

Many questions remain unanswered... or at least not answered as sufficiently as they could be. So... let's get to those questions. That's the purpose of this book!

I begin each chapter with a question that, in some form, has been posed to me. Some questions come from the Facebook group "The Uncontrolling Love of God Conversations" and other online discussion groups. Some come from lectures, as I've traveled across the U.S. and Europe. Some come from emails, social media, podcast interviews, conversations at coffee shops, and more.

I strive to keep each chapter short. And I try to write as plainly as possible. I hope you'll see how the uncontrolling love of God perspective you encountered in *God Can't* answers many other important questions!

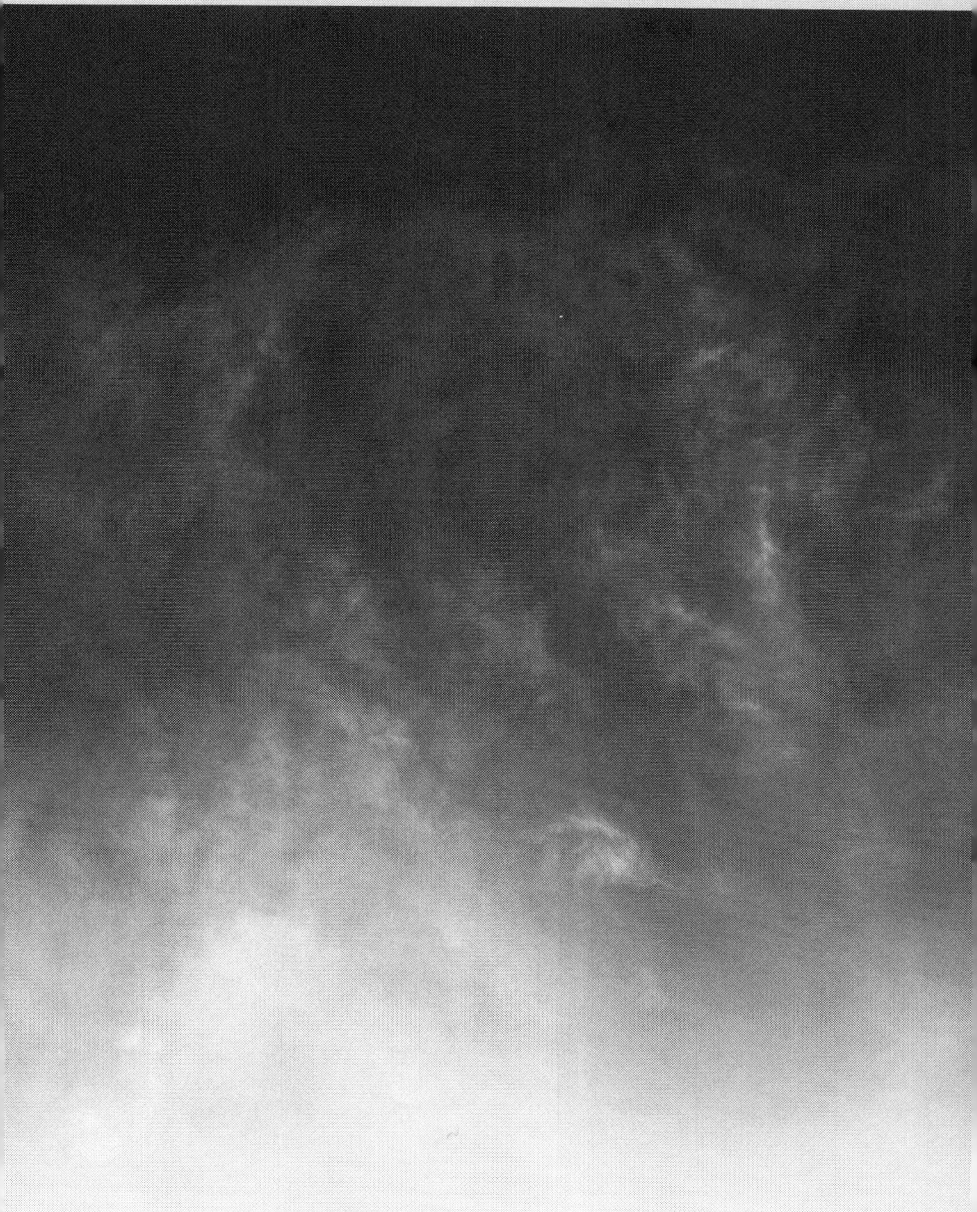

CHAPTER ONE

If God can't control, why pray?

I often hear this chapter's question. Readers of *God Can't* ask it in emails. I hear it from live audiences and podcast hosts. Many wonder what implications the uncontrolling love view has for prayer.

I appreciate this question. It shows that readers take seriously these theological ideas and want to explore their consequences. Many readers want to integrate *God Can't* ideas into their devotional lives and ways of living.

Prayer takes many forms, of course. The question framing this chapter falls under what many call "petitionary prayer." This involves asking God to do something. If God can't single-handedly control others to fix some problem or grant some wish, we might wonder why we should ask.

I spend most of this chapter exploring petitionary prayer. But near the end, I talk about what it means to pray in thanks, praise, and worship. The uncontrolling love of God view has positive implications for these forms of prayer too.

A CONTROLLING GOD AND A CORONAVIRUS VICTIM

Before answering this chapter's question, let me look at two alternative views of God and prayer. Each has negative implications for understanding petitionary prayer believers seldom realize.

To help us see what these alternative views of prayer entail, let's take the hypothetical case of Tim. As I write this book, Coronavirus/COVID-19 is killing hundreds of thousands of people and causing widespread harm. Let's suppose Tim has contracted the virus and wants us to pray for his health.

What prayers make sense?

Some people believe God controls absolutely everything. This is the "All God" view I mentioned in *God Can't*. It claims God does everything, because God is the omnicause. "God is sovereignly in control," say people who embrace this view.

The All God view rejects the idea we're genuinely free. God predetermines every moment of every creature. Most All God advocates believe God predestined all things from the foundation of the universe. And the God who predestines can foreknow everything that will happen.

So... if a person believes God controls everything, what does this mean we should say when praying for Tim?

The All God view says God caused the Coronavirus. It's God's will. Most who affirm this view believe God predestined the Coronavirus to kill, wreak havoc in the world, and sicken millions. Before the foundation of the world, God decided the virus would sicken Tim in particular. It's all part of God's meticulous blueprint.

If I believed the All God view, I could not bring myself to petition God. I would not pray for Tim. Here's why...

Petitionary prayer involves asking God to do something in the future. But the God who predetermined everything can't respond to such prayers. The future is already settled, and what will occur has already decided. If God predetermined Tim to contract the virus, my prayers make no difference to helping him. Asking God to do something new makes no sense.

In fact, my request for Tim's healing seems to oppose God's will. From the All God perspective, after all, God wanted Tim to be sick. And acting against God's will is, by definition, sin. Praying for Tim would be sinning!

I can't get inspired to ask something of a God for whom my actions make no difference. Besides, if the All God view is true that God wills everything, God wills that I can't get inspired to pray for Tim!

THE CONVENTIONAL GOD AND CORONAVIRUS VICTIM

Most people I know don't believe the All God view. Most believe they act freely, at least sometimes. Most think the future has not been predestined, even if they say God (mysteriously) knows everything that will occur. This leads to our second view of God and prayer.

The second view assumes what I call the "Conventional" view of God. People who believe in the Conventional view think God singlehandedly fixes things from time to time. But they think God usually allows the free processes of existence and free creatures to exert influence too.

Many people who identify as "classical Arminians" embrace this view of prayer. It says God can and sometimes does singlehandedly bring about results, cure people, stop evil, and so on. God foreknows everything that will ever occur without determining all of it. This God doesn't control everything but sometimes controls some things.

So, does this view make sense when praying for Tim?

Not really. The Conventional God is allegedly perfectly loving, has controlling power, and knows in advance everything that will ever occur. This God could heal Tim without our prayers, co-operation, medicine, or creaturely influences. And yet... this God rarely heals. Tim suffers from a virus the Conventional God fore-knew and could stop singlehandedly but has refused to do so.

Conventional theology implies God sometimes requires prayer to get him off his butt and do what's loving. Believers must beg, plead, or twist God's arm to get good results. But if Tim is not healed, he'll wonder if God has abandoned him, is punishing him, or this allows evil to teach a lesson. It's confusing.

If God loves everyone and everything and can singlehand-edly fix anything, why do we need to ask for help? Wouldn't this God automatically fix what is fixable? And if God fore-knows with certainty what will occur, petitionary prayer can-not change an already foreknown and therefore settled future.

MY DAUGHTER IS DROWNING

To explain why petitionary prayer makes little sense if the Conventional view is true, let me give an illustration.

Suppose I'm out with my family at a lake, and we're enjoy-ing a scorching summer afternoon. I look up from reading and see one of my daughters in the lake. In just a few seconds, I realize my daughter is drowning! Her head is bobbing up and down, and her arms are flailing. She's gasping for air!

Suppose I could jump in and rescue my daughter. I'm a decent swimmer, and it's likely I could save her life. But suppose I say, "She hasn't asked for help. She's not crying out, 'Help me, Dad.' So, I won't rescue her until she asks." Or suppose I say, "I'm not seeing anyone else begging me to save her. Unless 10 people ask, I will not leave the beach!"

No one would think I was a loving father if I could have rescued my drowning daughter but refused because I didn't hear her ask. No one would say, "She didn't ask for help, so he didn't help. That was the loving thing to do." Nor would anyone think I was loving if I waited for 10 people to ask me to help.

The Conventional view portrays God as having the ability to rescue singlehandedly but not always doing so unless we ask. It portrays God as metaphorically sitting back, arms folded, waiting for us to pray, or pray enough, before jumping in to help. Or it portrays God as waiting until a prayer chain of enough people intercede.

The Conventional God could singlehandedly heal Tim, prevent his illness, and fix just about anything. But for some mysterious reason, this God sometimes needs to be asked.

The Conventional view can't portray God as consistently loving. The God who could singlehandedly prevent evil but waits for us to ask is not a God of perfect love. A loving God who can save singlehandedly wouldn't require us to beg, plead, or petition 352 times before healing Tim.

PETITIONARY PRAYER AND THE UNCONTROLLING GOD

Petitionary prayer makes more sense in the uncontrolling love perspective. It assumes a relational view: God gives and receives in a relational world with relational creatures.

To many people, it's obviously true that creation influences God. That's the general view of God portrayed in the Bible, and it fits what many believers think today. The God who is angry at sin or blessed by praise is One whom creatures affect.

It surprises many to discover theologians of yesteryear disagreed. These thinkers believed God was unaffected by what happens in our lives and in the world. They said God was "impassible," to use the classic language. This means God is not compassionate in the way we understand compassion. It also means our prayers make no difference to God, because according to this view, God is not relational.

The uncontrolling love perspective fits the way most people pray, because most believe their prayers may affect God. God not only affects us and influences all creation moment by moment, we and all creation affect God. From the uncontrolling love view, petitionary prayer affects God. This is the first point for understanding prayer in a *God Can't* perspective.

The idea creatures are relational is the second important aspect for understanding petitionary prayer from a *God Can't* perspective. Creation is interconnected; action in one place affects those in others. My actions affect you; your actions affect me. Those actions may primarily be physical or mainly mental. But everything we do — including our prayers — affects ourselves and the world.

In the past, I would need to illustrate the idea creation is interconnected. But nearly everyone acknowledges this reality today. Our decisions affect our bodies, friends and family, societies, and the environment. Praying is an activity.

When we combine the idea that prayer affects God with the idea prayer affects ourselves and others, we can see how prayer makes a difference to an uncontrolling God and to the world.

Added to this is the truth that life moves on moment by moment. The past is complete, the present is becoming what it will be, and the future is open. God relates with us moment by moment as the Living Lover of history.[1]

Our prayer in one moment influences what is possible in the next. And the God who is present to all receives our actions each moment. This means our prayers open up new avenues for God to work. Fresh opportunities emerge each moment because we prayed. Prayer generates new relationships, data, forces, factors, and information for God to respond to when deciding how to act in the next moment. Because we pray, God may have alternative paths to operate in, new cooperative agents to work with, and new opportunities to influence us and others.

Prayer changes history.

When I say prayer influences God and the world, I'm **not** saying prayer controls others or creation. I'm **not** saying our prayers guarantee the results we want. And I'm **not** saying prayer allows God to control. Petitionary prayer doesn't "turbo-charge" God to determine results singlehandedly. Our prayers are not coins in a vending machine that automatically dispenses the drink we want.

Prayer makes a difference, but it doesn't control.

This point is so important that I want to emphasize it. An uncontrolling love view says petitionary prayer makes a difference without fully determining others. It says our prayers affect God without saying prayers make it possible for God to determine others fully. It says praying opens new possibilities God can use in the next moment, without saying those possibilities *guarantee* the rescuing, healing, or blessing we seek. Prayer can be a factor in the good that occurs, but it doesn't guarantee it.

In one sense, the uncontrolling love view fits what most believers think about God's response to their prayers. Most doubt, for instance, their prayers *force* God to control. Few pray, "Dear God, *force* Uncle Joe to become loving." Few pray, "God, control Jennifer to *make* her become a Christian." Most people think God is uncontrollable, so our prayers don't force God to do anything. I agree.

I think God is both uncontrollable and uncontrolling. We can't control God, and there's no sense trying. God is uncontrollable. But God can't control us, others, or anything in creation. God is uncontrolling. God loves everyone and everything, so God can't control anyone or anything.

"Controlling love" is an oxymoron.

PRAYING WITH TIM

Let's return to Tim, the Coronavirus victim. I want to spell out concretely what petitionary prayer might look like in his case.

Let's imagine Tim hospitalized by Coronavirus symptoms, and I've been asked to pray with him. What should I say? How might I pray in a way that makes sense if I believe God can't control?

Acknowledge Suffering

After taking the necessary precautions, I approach Tim to pray. Typically, my first thought is to vocalize the problem. I acknowledge Tim's suffering. I might say,

*Loving God, we are in this hospital because Tim is suf-
fering. You know the pain and struggle he endures,
and we know it too. This virus is wracking Tim's body
and affecting him negatively in so many ways.*

Before moving to the second part of my prayer, let me analyze the first. Acknowledging Tim's suffering doesn't inform
God that Tim is sick, as if God was previously unaware. God
knows the situation better than Tim and I do, in fact, even better than physicians and nurses. God isn't clueless.

Acknowledging this suffering aloud is doing something
new, however. Tim is presumably listening. Often part of the
healing process is knowing others empathize with us, see
us, hear us, or have some understanding of what we endure.
Something powerful can occur when sufferers know others
perceive their pain and suffer with them.

In addition, Tim's mind influences his body. Humans have
a psychosomatic unity, which means the mental affects the
physical, and the physical affects the mental. My words of
acknowledgement and empathy not only influence Tim's
thought patterns, they influence his ill body. My words and
their influence provide God extra causal factors God might use
in future work with Tim. My prayer, in other words, is already
making a difference.

Acknowledge God's Work to Heal

The second aspect of my prayer acknowledges God's activity.

*We acknowledge your efforts to heal Tim. We believe
you are the Great Physician. You are working right now*

to the greatest extent possible to bring about healing.
Thank you for your healing activities.

Let's analyze this second aspect. If the uncontrolling love of God view is correct, God always works to heal to the greatest extent possible (for details on this, see chapter three of *God Can't*). My saying, "We acknowledge your efforts to heal" isn't telling God something new about what God has been doing. It's not like God thinks, "Oh, so that's what I've been up to lately. Who knew?!"

Acknowledging God's work to heal does something new at this moment, however. My prayer tells Tim something new or reminds him of something he's known: God wants to heal. God doesn't sit around twiddling thumbs waiting to be asked. God wants to heal everyone and everything, and God always works to heal to the greatest extent possible. Acknowledging God as a healer is important for Tim's mental state. His mental state affects the state of his body. So, my saying God is already working to heal may provide new possibilities and avenues for God in the healing process.

Acknowledge Opposition to Healing

Let's move to the third phase of my prayer.

We know you, God, are facing forces and factors —
specifically, a virus — opposing the healing you want.
We know principalities and powers of various types
sometimes run counter to the good you want in our
lives and in creation.

Let's analyze this third phase. In this, I'm acknowledging aloud God doesn't have the power to erase all opposition by absolute fiat or decree. I'm endorsing the uncontrolling love view and assuming God can't singlehandedly prevent evil.

Tim might interpret "forces, factors, principalities, and powers" as a reference to demonic beings. He might think these words refer to natural causes. I specifically identified the virus, but his interpretation depends largely on his worldview. I probably won't engage Tim on whether demonic agents or natural factors caused the virus.[2] But I want to put in his mind the idea that God works to heal but faces obstacles, opposition, and resistance.

This third aspect of the prayer is crucial. I don't want Tim to think God has the controlling power that many claim. Many believers pray in ways that imply God can singlehandedly fix all problems. People who suffer like Tim, therefore, expect unilateral healing... but are often not healed.

Most of us know firsthand the problems that come with thinking God can singlehandedly heal. We who are ill, injured, abused, or suffering may wonder if God truly loves us. We wonder if God is punishing or has abandoned us. We wonder if, in some mysterious way, our pain and suffering are an unfortunate part of some divine plan. And so on.

It's crucial to believe God cannot singlehandedly overcome opposition to God's healing work.

Commit to Cooperating with God

Let's move to the fourth phase of my prayer for Tim. In this phase, I pray words of commitment:

At this moment, God, we commit ourselves to cooperate with your healing work. Tim does, and so do I. We commit to following what we believe is best in this situation, such as heeding the counsel of physicians, nurses, and health care workers. We want to sleep well and drink fluids. We commit to cooperating with you to fight this illness.

In our analysis of this fourth phase, it should be clear these words are explicit commitments to cooperate with God's healing. We're not just providing new information. We're committing to do our part in the healing work. Commitment to cooperate doesn't guarantee instantaneous healing or even healing at all. But Tim's present promise and future actions have an actual effect on his body and mental state.

I've already mentioned the psychosomatic interaction between Tim's mind and body. In future chapters, I will offer a philosophical framework for making sense of this. Here I simply want to say Tim's mind doesn't control his body. A commitment to cooperate with God's healing doesn't mean Tim's cells, organs, and other bodily members will automatically reject the virus. Commitments to cooperate bring instantaneous healing on only the rarest of occasions. And when they do, it wasn't the person's cooperation alone that cured the illness.

Our minds affect our bodies, and our bodies affect our minds. But no aspect of ourselves controls other aspects. Sometimes our minds cooperate with God fully, and yet our bodies do not. Sometimes external factors cause us harm that neither our bodies nor minds can resist. And sometimes our bodily members cooperate with God when we mentally do not cooperate. We are complex creatures in a complex world.

Asking God for Help

I'm now to the part of the prayer we normally consider petition. At this point, I might say,

> Help us know how we might cooperate with your healing work. Give us insight. We also ask that you comfort Tim as much as is possible in this fight for healing. We seek your guidance.

These words present requests of God. But the previous aspects of my prayer have also been making a difference to God and creation. In one sense, all prayer is petitionary, if we understand "petition" as "having an impact upon" God. All of life is petitionary prayer, in that sense, because *everything* we do influences God's experience. I think about this when pondering the Apostle Paul's recommendation to "pray without ceasing" (1 Thess. 5:17).

We usually think of petitionary prayer as a series of specific requests. The specific requests I'm making for Tim pertain to what he needs. I'm asking God to give us wisdom and insight on how to cooperate with God's healing work. And I'm asking God to comfort Tim. I could add additional petitions, depending on the situation. God responds to all our requests by calling various agents, factors, and forces to join in God's work.

When petitioning God, I don't assume giving wisdom, comfort, insight, inspiration, and so on involves God controlling us and others. I'm not asking God to do activities only possible for a controlling God. God's responses to petitionary prayer involve creaturely causes. Not only can we humans cooperate with the Spirit, other creatures and entities can too, given their abilities.

Acknowledge God's Love

I conclude my prayer by thanking God for loving Tim:

Whether in sickness or health, in sorrow or joy, we believe you love Tim. You love all creation. And in love, you work for our good in all things, God. Thanks for your loving kindness and compassion.

Amen.

When I leave the hospital, I want Tim to realize God cares deeply about him. The uncontrolling love of God view of prayer places love first. It says God desires and acts for Tim's well-being and the well-being of all creation. And that involves God's compassionate care.

I also want to leave the hospital knowing I did not give Tim the impression God can singlehandedly cure him. His partnership with God can make a difference, as well as the cooperation of other people, factors, and actors. This collaboration doesn't guarantee healing, because other factors may oppose God's work for Tim's health. But cooperation makes a difference in the work of healing.[3]

THANKSGIVING

I turn now from petition to prayers of gratitude. The *God Can't* view has positive implications for how we think about thanksgiving. If this view is correct, thanking an uncontrolling God makes sense.

Let's take the Thanksgiving holiday meal as a case study for prayers of gratitude.

Each November, Americans gather with family or friends to celebrate the Thanksgiving holiday. Words of thanks sometimes enter the public news or get expressed at civic gatherings. It's natural to wonder what people believe when they say, "Thank you, God."

One group of people doesn't believe in God. Many of them feel thankful, but their Thanksgiving language has no ultimate Referent. In their view, no Divine Being exists to which their gratitude ultimately points. Giving thanks to God may a way to admit they've been recipients of goodness. Although these unbelievers may say, "Thank you, God," their disbelief a Being exists to whom they should be grateful makes their statement confusing.

Those who say God controls everything — the All God people — express gratitude at Thanksgiving. The God they believe in directly or indirectly controls everything. In their Thanksgiving prayer, they can say, "Thank you, God, for ____," and insert any event. Such events might be supremely joyful or utterly horrific. The God who controls everything is responsible for every act of respect and rape, for peace and pain, for havens or holocausts. Most All God prayers focus on the good. Reminding All God advocates that their God causes evil dampens the holiday spirit!

Conventional theology advocates also pray at Thanksgiving. They usually reject the idea God causes evil, but they claim God allows it. When they're giving thanks, they try to sidestep the theological problems that come with saying God allows evil.

They'll blame free agents or natural forces and ignore the question of why a God who can singlehandedly stop evil permits unnecessary suffering. The God who can control others failed to prevent the dastardly deeds we endure.

When people who accept the Conventional view of God pray at Thanksgiving, they *could* insert any event into "Thank you, God, for _____." The God of Conventional theology gets ultimate credit or blame for causing or allowing all things.

Thanksgiving prayers make more sense in the uncontrolling love of God perspective. Advocates of this view thank the God who always gives freedom, agency, or existence to creatures and creation. God presents a spectrum of possibilities to each creature in each moment.

God is the gracious source for all that's good.

The uncontrolling God actively loves, moment by moment, by providing, inspiring, empowering, and interacting with creation. And this God calls all creatures to respond in love. The genuine evil in the world results from the responses creatures make contrary to God's calls, or from the natural accidents and free processes of reality.

In her Thanksgiving prayer, an advocate of the uncontrolling love view can say every good and perfect gift originates in God. An active but uncontrolling God is the source of goodness and blessing but can't singlehandedly prevent evil. The good we enjoy involves creaturely responses to God's gracious action.

The uncontrolling love view supports our urge to thank creatures at Thanksgiving. Most believers thank one another from time to time, as if they intuitively know creatures join with God to do good. It's right to thank God for acting as the ultimate source of goodness, but we should also thank those who cooperate with God. We can thank God and the cook!

The more we realize how interrelated the universe is and how much God loves in an uncontrolling way, the more we understand how widely we are indebted. A Thanksgiving meal is possible because of God's action, a chef or chefs, farmers, those who transport food, those who make the plates, tables, and homes we use when celebrating, and so many more. God inspires goodness throughout all creation.

We have many reasons to be thankful... and many to thank!

PRAYERS OF PRAISE AND WORSHIP

I conclude with a few comments on prayers of praise and worship. These activities have been the center of how believers understand God's activity. Believers express prayers of praise and worship both corporately and individually. A perfectly loving, powerful, and beautiful God is worthy of praise and worship!

Unfortunately, many prayers of worship or songs of praise place priority upon God's power to the detriment of God's love. God is powerful, but I often hear language that frames God's love in light of power rather than the opposite. I could point to examples in "low church" worship choruses and in the "high church" prayers of praise.

Many worship songs stress sovereignty when speaking of God's glory. "God is in control," they proclaim. "God orchestrates every lightning strike and falling leaf." Some songs ask God to "take my will" or say God's ways are "irresistible." Taken literally, many worship songs assume God is or could be controlling.

I can't worship a God who could singlehandedly control but chooses not to prevent evil. By "worship," I mean give whole-hearted trust and devotion. I can't whole-heartedly trust a God who could prevent evil but chooses not to do so. I can't be entirely devoted to an inconsistently loving deity. It's more than an intellectual inability. My inability to worship a controlling God is visceral!

The idea we should praise controlling power is deeply ingrained in most of us. When some hear that I can't worship a controlling God, they respond in shock. Some wonder, "Is a God who *can't* control even worth worshipping?"

I respond to this rhetorical question by saying my worship is unreserved and whole-hearted. I worship without qualms a God who loves everyone and everything but can't control anyone or anything. Without crossing my fingers, I stand in amazement. As I see it, God's glory derives primarily from God's steadfast love.

The question of worship has implications for ethics. A full exploration, like many of these topics, requires a book-length response. But let me say a few words.

What we think God is like affects how we think we ought to live. If we think God is uncontrolling and loves at all times and places, this can motivate us to imitate God by loving in an uncontrolling way at all times and places. If we think God is in control, calls the shots, and is in charge, it's natural to think we ought at least sometimes to be in control, call the shots, and be in charge. Trying to control others leads to ruin, however. An ethics of uncontrolling love says we ought to influence others for good without controlling them.[4]

The uncontrolling love perspective has powerful implications for how we ought to act!

IF GOD CAN'T CONTROL, WHY PRAY?

Prayer comes in many forms. We should engage in petitionary prayer, because it affects God and creation. Our prayers open new possibilities and opportunities for God and others. Prayer neither controls God nor makes God able to control others. We can't control an uncontrollable God, and an uncontrolling God can't control us. But prayer makes an actual difference to the Creator and to creation.

The uncontrolling love of God perspective provides a satisfying overall framework to understand prayer. I'm motivated to pray when I believe God cannot control but lovingly influences all. My inclination to pray in thanks and praise makes sense from a *God Can't* perspective. It makes far less sense if God can or does control others.

As I prayed this morning, I used a breathing exercise. I imagined breathing into my lungs God's loving presence. I inhaled. I then imagined breathing out love for others, God, myself, and all creation. I exhaled. I inhaled God's empowering love and exhaled my response of love. This is a symbolic expression of what I think literally occurs, as God loves moment-by-moment and calls for response.

I hope this view of an uncontrolling God influenced by our petitions inspires you to pray.

ENDNOTES

Preface

1. Thomas Jay Oord, *God Can't! How to Believe in God and Love after Tragedy, Abuse, and Other Evils* (Grasmere, Id.: SacraSage, 2019); Spanish Translation: *Dios No Puede: Como Creer en Dios y el Amor Despues de la Tragedia, el Abuso y Otros Males,* Lemuel Sandoval, trans. (SacraSage, 2019); German Translation: *GOTT kann das nicht! Wie man trotz Tragödien, Missbrauch oder anderem Unheil den Glauben an Gott und Seine Liebe bewahrt,* Michael Trenkel and Dirk Weisensee, trans. (SacraSage, 2019).

Introduction: *God Can't* is Helping People

1. For chapter-length stories from those who have been helped by the uncontrolling love view, see L Michaels, ed. *What about Us? Stories of Uncontrolling Love* (Grasmere, Id.: SacraSage, 2019).

2. See *The Uncontrolling Love of God* (Downers Grove, Ill.: IVP Academic, 2015), ch. 7.

3. See Jürgen Moltmann, "God's Kenosis in the Creation and Consummation of the World," in *The Work of Love: Creation as Kenosis,* ed. John C. Polkinghorne (Grand Rapids: Eerdmans, 2001), 146.

4. Bradford McCall explores this idea in relation to emergence, *A Modern Relation of Theology and Science Assisted by Kenosis and Emergence* (Wipf and Stock, 2018).

5. On this, see my essay "Genuine (but Limited) Freedom for Creatures and for a God of Love" In *Neuroscience and Free Will,* James Walters and Philip Clayton, eds. (Eugene, Or.: Pickwick, 2020).

6. Lisa Michaels, et. al., eds. *Uncontrolling Love: Essays Exploring the Love of God, with Introductions by Thomas Jay Oord* (San Diego, CA: SacraSage, 2017).

1. If God can't control, why pray?

1. Christopher Fisher defends the open view that supports this claim by exploring various biblical passages. See his *God is Open: Examining the Open Theism of the Biblical Authors* (CreateSpace, 2017).

2. Greg Boyd has used the idea of Satan and demons when formulating his open and relational theology. Among his many books on the subject, see *Satan and the Problem of Evil: Constructing a Trinitarian Warfare Theodicy* (Downers Grove, IL: InterVarsity Press, 2001);

3. For outstanding books on prayer among the many available, see Mark Karris, *Divine Echoes: Reconciling Prayer with the Uncontrolling Love of God* (Orange, California: Quior, 2018); Marjorie Suchocki, *In God's Presence: Theological Re lections on Prayer* (St. Louis, Mo.: Chalice, 1996); Bruce Epperly, *Praying with Process Theology: Spiritual Practices for Personal and Planetary Healing* (River Lane, 2017).

4. Philip Clayton lays out some of these implications in *Transforming Christian Theology: For Church and Society* (Philadelphia: Fortress, 2009).

For the remainder of this book, visit your favorite bookseller...

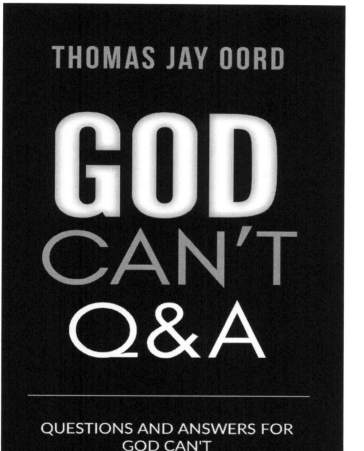

The
Uncontrolling
Love *of* God

AN OPEN AND RELATIONAL
ACCOUNT OF PROVIDENCE

Contents

7
<hr>

The Essential Kenosis Model of Providence

W^e began our efforts to make sense of life by looking at true stories of genuine evil. In each account, aspects of randomness and free will were present. We also encountered unsatisfying explanations for why a loving and powerful God did not prevent these horrific events. We need persuasive answers to life's puzzling questions.

Genuinely random, chance and accidental events occur often in the world. From quantum events to genetic mutations to human interactions and beyond, existence bubbles with randomness. We also find structure, order and consistency in creation. Lawlike regularities persist in everyday life and the world explored by science. Existence as we know it depends upon regularities. Neither absolute randomness nor absolute regularity, however, reigns absolutely. The lawlike regularity of the world combined with spontaneous randomness provides a context for both creative novelty and faithful reliability.

Humans (and perhaps other complex creatures) act freely although all creaturely freedom is limited. Most if not all humans have libertarian free will, even if some deny it. We may not find full-blown freedom among simpler entities and less complex organisms, but we do find self-organization and in some a measure of agency. Freedom and agency used wrongly cause genuine evil. But evils can also have random causes.

Life is not all about evil. We encounter much good in life too. It makes sense to me and to many others that a good God is the source of goodness. Explanations of existence that include a prominent role for God are more satisfying overall. In fact, it makes sense that God uses creaturely free choices and random events in ongoing creating and providential activity. However, believers are right to wonder why this good God fails to prevent genuine evils that free choices and random events cause.

Those who believe in God offer various theories—models of providence—to account for divine action. Providence models that deny randomness and freedom do not correspond with life as we know it. Models that say God is impersonal, uninvolved or unaffected by creation cannot account well for religious experiences, goodness and love, or sacred Scripture. Models that say God sometimes entirely controls others or, in principle, could do so fail to provide plausible answers to the problem of evil. Models of providence appealing to utter mystery or an inscrutable divine will are especially unhelpful. Although we will never understand God completely, we need a plausible model of providence if we are to make sense of reality.

Open and relational theology offers helpful answers to life's questions. It affirms genuine randomness and lawlike regularity. This theology embraces self-organization, agency and libertarian free will. Open and relational theology believes that values are real, including genuine evil; that good God is good; and that it is possible for creatures to do what is good. The active and relational God of this perspective knows all that can be known, but the future remains authentically open to both Creator and creatures.

Even though open and relational theologies are attractive, unresolved questions remain. One of the most thorough expositions of open and relational theology to date, for instance, fails to solve the problem of evil. This version of open and relational theology fails largely because it says God permits pointless evil. It considers sovereignty, rather than love, to come first logically in God's nature.

In previous chapters, I promised a version of open and relational theology I call essential kenosis. I said this theology would answer remaining questions and provide a model of providence that includes randomness and regularity, free will and necessity, goodness and evil, and more. This model would emphasize that God loves all creation steadfastly because God's nature is uncontrolling love. And it would offer a plausible solution to the problem of evil.

It is time to make good on my promise.

KENOSIS

Let's begin with Jesus Christ and kenosis. The verb form of *kenōsis* appears about a half dozen times in the New Testament. One of the most discussed appearances comes in the apostle Paul's letter to believers in the city of Philippi. The text is powerful for what it says about God, Jesus and the way we ought to live.

Here is the Philippians text, including the verses surrounding *kenōsis*, to provide context for help in finding its meaning:

> Let each of you look not to your own interests, but to the interests of others. Let the same mind be in you that was in Christ Jesus,
>
> who, though he was in the form of God,
>   did not regard equality with God
>   as something to be exploited,
> but emptied himself [*ekenōsen* = kenosis],
>   taking the form of a slave,
>   being born in human likeness.
> And being found in human form,
>   he humbled himself
>   and became obedient to the point of death—
>   even death on a cross.
> Therefore God also highly exalted him
>   and gave him the name
>   that is above every name,
> so that at the name of Jesus
>   every knee should bend,
>   in heaven and on earth and under the earth,
> and every tongue should confess
>   that Jesus Christ is Lord,
>   to the glory of God the Father.

Therefore, my beloved, just as you have always obeyed me, not only in
my presence, but much more now in my absence, work out your own
salvation with fear and trembling; for it is God who is at work in
you, enabling you both to will and to work for his good pleasure.
(Phil 2:4-13)

This passage begins with Paul's ethical instructions: look to the in-
terests of others, not your own. He points to Jesus Christ, who divinely
acts as the primary example of someone who expresses other-oriented
love. Jesus' love is evident, says Paul, in his diminished power and his
service to others. The weakness of the cross is an especially powerful
example of Jesus acting for the good of others.[1] God endorses Jesus'
other-oriented love, and God enables those who follow Jesus' example
to pursue salvation. Paul tells readers to pursue salvation earnestly.

All Scripture requires interpretation. Theologians interpret this
passage in various ways and apply it to various issues. When consid-
ering the meaning of *kenōsis*, theologians in previous centuries typically focused on the phrase just prior to *kenōsis* in this passage:
"[Jesus] did not regard equality with God as something to be exploited"
(Phil 2:6). They believed it provides clues for explaining Jesus' humanity and divinity.

At a fifth-century meeting in Chalcedon, Christian theologians
issued a statement saying Jesus Christ has two natures "communicated to" one person. Jesus is the God-human, said many who at-
tended the meeting. He is fully divine and fully human. These early
church leaders arrived at this view after rejecting other options for
understanding Jesus as the Christ.

Theologians thereafter pondered which divine attributes Jesus re-
tained in human life and which, apparently as a result of self-emptying,
he did not. The Chalcedonian creed offers little to no help in answering the specifics of this issue. Theologians today still ponder how
Jesus is both human and divine.[2]

---

[1]Jürgen Moltmann has become well known for this idea, and he explains it in *The Crucified God* (London: SCM Press, 1974).
[2]On the historical debate of kenosis and Jesus' two natures, see David Brown, *Divine Humanity:*

In recent decades, however, discussions of kenosis have shifted.[3] Instead of appealing to kenosis in the debate over which divine attributes Jesus possesses, theologians today use *kenosis* primarily to describe how Jesus *reveals* God's nature. Instead of imagining how God may have relinquished attributes when becoming incarnate, many now think Jesus' kenosis tells us who God is and how God acts.

The contemporary shift to thinking of kenosis as Jesus revealing God's nature moves theologians away from phrases in the passage preceding *kenōsis*. Following the lead of some biblical scholars, many theologians now read *kenōsis* primarily in light of phrases such as "taking the form of a slave," "humbled himself" and "death on a cross." These phrases immediately follow *kenōsis*, and they focus on Jesus' diminished power and service to others.[4] They suggest that God's power is essentially persuasive and vulnerable, not overpowering and aloof. We especially see God's noncoercive power revealed in the cross of Christ, which suggests that God's power is cruciform (see also 1 Cor 1:18-25).[5] Phrases in the Philippians passage describe forms of other-oriented love.

Kenosis and the Construction of a Christian Theology (Waco, TX: Baylor University Press, 2011); and Thomas R. Thompson, "Nineteenth-Century Kenotic Christology: Waxing, Waning and Weighing of a Quest for a Coherent Orthodoxy," in *Exploring the Kenotic Christology: The Self-Emptying of God*, ed. C. Stephen Evans (Vancouver: Regent College, 2006).

[3]Among recent helpful texts on kenosis, see Brown, *Divine Humanity*; Peter J. Colyer, *The Self-Emptying God: An Undercurrent in Christian Theology Helping the Relationship with Science* (Cambridge: Cambridge Scholars, 2013); C. Stephen Evans, ed., *Exploring Kenotic Christology: The Self-Emptying of God* (Vancouver: Regent College, 2006); and John C. Polkinghorne, ed., *The Work of Love: Creation as Kenosis* (Grand Rapids: Eerdmans, 2001).

[4]See the work of biblical scholars such as John Dominic Crossan and Jonathan Reed, *In Search of Paul: How Jesus's Apostle Opposed Rome's Empire with God's Kingdom* (San Francisco: HarperSanFrancisco, 2004), p. 290; James D. G. Dunn, *Christology in the Making: An Inquiry into the Origins of the Doctrine of the Incarnation*, 2nd ed. (London: SCM Press, 1989), p. 116; Michael J. Gorman, *Inhabiting the Cruciform God: Kenosis, Justification, and Theosis in Paul's Narrative Soteriology* (Grand Rapids: Eerdmans, 2009), chap. 1; Donald Macleod, *The Person of Christ*, Contours of Christian Theology (Leicester: Inter-Varsity Press, 1998), p. 215; Ralph P. Martin, *Carmen Christi: Philippians 2:5-11 in Recent Interpretation and in the Setting of Early Christian Worship*, rev. ed. (Grand Rapids: Eerdmans, 1983), p. 170; and N. T. Wright, *The Climax of the Covenant* (Minneapolis: Fortress, 1993), p. 84.

[5]For the relation between God's holiness and cruciformity, see Michael Gorman, "'You Shall Be Cruciform for I Am Cruciform': Paul's Trinitarian Reconstruction of Holiness," in *Holiness and Ecclesiology in the New Testament*, ed. Kent E. Brower and Andy Johnson (Grand Rapids: Eerdmans, 2007), pp. 148-66.

I follow the contemporary trend of interpreting kenosis primarily as Jesus' qualified power, other-orientation and servant love. This interpretation seems more fruitful overall than discussions about what might be communicated between Christ's two natures, although I think such discussions have their place. My interpretation also helps us consider God's essential power, in light of God's loving nature and orientation toward creation. Consequently, I refer to kenosis to talk not so much about how God became incarnate as to understand God's nature in light of incarnate love. For as the writer of Hebrews puts it, Jesus is the "exact representation of [God's] nature" (Heb 1:3 NASB).

We can know something about God's nature in the light of Jesus' kenotic love.

Theologians also debate how best to translate the word *kenōsis*. While most believe it tells us something true about God, no one knows precisely what the word means. *Kenōsis* sits in the midst of what biblical scholars believe to be a poem or hymn, and this genre allows for an especially wide range of interpretations. Scholars interpret *kenōsis* variously as "self-emptying," "self-withdrawing," "self-limiting" or "self-giving."

Some of these translations are less helpful than others. "Self-emptying," for instance, does not make much sense if taken literally. To say God is emptied sounds like deity is a container whose contents pour out. This is not the personal language of love, and love seems the central point of the passage. Biblical scholar Gordon Fee, for instance, says the idea that God self-empties is at best metaphorical because "the suggestion that Christ 'emptied himself' *of* something is quite foreign to Paul's own concern."[6] Kenosis is not "a divestiture of something," says biblical scholar Michael Gorman.[7] Relational language, rather than container language, is more helpful if kenosis pertains primarily to love.

---

[6]Gordon D. Fee, "The New Testament and Kenosis Christology," in *Exploring Kenotic Christology: The Self-Emptying of God*, ed. C. Stephen Evans (Vancouver: Regent College, 2006), p. 29. See also Gordon D. Fee, *Paul's Letter to the Philippians* (Grand Rapids: Eerdmans, 1995), p. 210.
[7]Gorman, *Inhabiting the Cruciform God*, p. 22.

Jürgen Moltmann sometimes uses "self-withdrawing" to describe kenosis. God "withdrew himself into himself in order to make room for the world," says Moltmann. In kenosis, God "distances himself" from the world "to concede space for the presence of creation."[8] In this, says Moltmann, "the omnipotent and omnipresent God withdraws his presence and restricts his power."[9] This involves "a restriction of God's omnipotence, omnipresence, and omniscience for the sake of conceding room to live to those he has created."[10]

Moltmann's intent is laudable because he seeks to account for divine love and creaturely freedom.[11] But self-withdrawing language is problematic for several reasons. Saying God withdraws from space, if taken literally, implies God is no longer omnipresent. Saying God self-restricts knowledge suggests God does not know all that is knowable, which negates omniscience. Saying divine power is self-restricted suggests God is not doing all God could do, which opens self-withdrawing theology up to the criticism that it promotes a deity not fully engaged with creation. Understanding kenosis as withdrawing introduces serious complications.

Perhaps the most common understanding of kenosis is that God, out of love, voluntarily self-limits for the sake of others. Jeff Pool describes this view of kenosis as "volitional divine self-limitation" because "God restricts the divine self."[12] Vincent Brümmer affirms voluntary self-limitation and says God's power does not derive from a "limitation or a dependence which is imposed on God from outside."[13] Polkinghorne says "divine power is deliberately self-

---

[8]Jürgen Moltmann, "God's Kenosis in the Creation and Consummation of the World," in *The Work of Love: Creation as Kenosis*, ed. John C. Polkinghorne (Grand Rapids: Eerdmans, 2001), p. 146.

[9]Jürgen Moltmann, *God in Creation* (London: SCM Press, 1985), p. 87.

[10]Moltmann, "God's Kenosis," p. 147.

[11]Moltmann often unites his understanding of kenosis with the notion of zimzum, a concept he explores in several books. Zimsum is God withdrawing into Godself. It's God's self-limitation for the other (*God in Creation* [San Francisco: Harper & Row, 1985], p. 86). See Anna Case-Winters's critique in *Reconstructing a Christian Theology of Nature* (Burlington, VT: Ashgate, 2007), chap. 7.

[12]Jeff B. Pool, *Divine Vulnerability and Creation*, vol. 1 of *God's Wounds: Hermeneutic of the Christian Symbol of Divine Suffering* (Cambridge: James Clarke, 2009), p. 139.

[13]Vincent Brümmer, *What Are We Doing When We Pray? A Philosophical Enquiry* (London: SCM

limited."[14] Notice that self-limitation in each of these cases is thought to be voluntary. God essentially retains the capacity to control others, but God willingly self-restricts.

Several problems emerge when we think of kenosis as God's voluntary self-limitation, and we have mentioned these in previous chapters.[15] The primary one is that voluntary self-limitation says God does not always use for good the power God essentially possesses.[16] We see this plainly when, for instance, Polkinghorne spells out what voluntary self-limitation means for questions of evil. "God does not will the act of a murderer or the destructive force of an earthquake," he says, "but allows both to happen in a world in which divine power is deliberately self-limited to allow causal space for creatures."[17]

Theologians who understand kenosis as voluntary self-limitation believe God voluntarily chooses not to prevent genuine evil.[18] Instead, God permits it. We are right to think, however, that the God who voluntarily self-limits ought to become un-self-limited, for the sake of love, to prevent genuine evil. In other words, kenosis understood as voluntarily self-limitation leaves God culpable for failing to prevent genuine evil. Kenosis as voluntary self-limitation fails to make good sense in light of genuine evil.

These three interpretations of kenosis—self-emptying, self-withdrawing or voluntary self-limitation—present significant problems. Some don't match relational notions of other-oriented love, which seem the overall point of the passage. Others imply that God is not present in all places or not as influential as God could be. And each

---

Press, 1984), p. 67.

[14]John C. Polkinghorne, "Kenotic Creation and Divine Action," in *The Work of Love: Creation as Kenosis*, ed. John C. Polkinghorne (Grand Rapids: Eerdmans, 2001), p. 102.

[15]The voluntary divine self-limitation approach aligns with the voluntarist rather than the intellectualist/nature tradition of philosophical theology. I explored these traditions briefly in chapter two.

[16]Anna Case-Winters argues similarly in *God's Power: Traditional Understandings and Contemporary Challenges* (Louisville, KY: Westminster John Knox, 1990), p. 204.

[17]Polkinghorne, "Kenotic Creation and Divine Action," p. 102.

[18]One of the better scholarly examinations of divine power in relation to evil is Atle Otteson Søvik, *The Problem of Evil and the Power of God: On the Coherence and Authenticity of Some Christian Theodicies with Different Understandings of God's Power* (Oslo: Unipub AS, 2009).

leaves the problem of evil unresolved. These portrayals of kenosis offer little help for understanding the relation between God's power and love in the face of evil.

Although no translation is perfect, the most helpful rendering of *kenōsis* may be "self-giving." Interpreting kenosis as self-giving and therefore others-empowering love has the advantage of fitting well the opening context of the Philippians passage, which emphasizes acting for the good of others. It also fits well the culmination of the passage, which says God enables creatures to follow Jesus' example by living lives of love. Enabling involves the self acting to empower others.

Kenōsis translated as "self-giving, others-empowering love" corresponds well with passages found throughout Scripture. Readers often find passages saying God's action is necessary for creaturely life and love, for instance. I could offer many examples, but the John puts it plainly: "We love because he first loved us" (1 Jn 4:19). John also says, "apart from [God] you can do nothing" (Jn 15:5), which implies that we rely on God's gift of agency. Although in a flair of hyperbole, Paul illustrates this when he says, "I can do all things through [Christ] who strengthens me" (Phil 4:13). God's creating, life-giving and love-empowering presence is required for all creation, says Paul, for in God "we live and move and have our being" (Acts 17:28). This love is revealed most profoundly in the cross. As Victor Furnish puts it, "the saving power of God revealed in the cross is the power of God's self-giving love."[19] A major advantage of understanding kenosis as self-giving, others-empower love, in fact, is that the theme appears in various forms throughout the Old and New Testaments, even if the word *kenōsis* is not used.

Kenosis as self-giving, others-empowering love must be clarified, however. Divine self-giving does not mean creatures actually become divine. When self-giving, God does not bestow divinity upon creatures thereby making them deities. While humans can become Christ-like and can bear the divine image (2 Pet 1:4), they remain

---

[19]Victor Paul Furnish, *The Theology of the First Letter to the Corinthians* (Cambridge: Cambridge University Press, 1999), p. 74.

creatures. God's self-giving does not convert creatures into gods.

Understanding God to possess self-giving, others-empowering love also does not mean God loses the divine self after loving others. Self-giving does not make God literally selfless. This point seems important to mention because when creatures become "imitators God, as beloved children, and live in love" (Eph 5:1-2), they retain their selves in this loving. Buddhists, not Christians, seek the literal loss of self. God doesn't lose the divine self when giving.

Kenosis as self-giving, others-empowering love is also supports healthy self-love. Self-giving love only sometimes involves self-sacrifice. Some Christians have unfortunately believed that self-giving love opposes acting for one's own well-being. By contrast, kenosis as self-giving love supports the truth that self-love has a legitimate place in Christian ethics. Love decenters self-interest, but it does not destroy it.

The context in which we find *kenōsis* shows Paul's concern that his readers promote what many call "the common good." Self-giving kenosis promotes overall well-being. In addition, those who imitate Christ's actions to promote well-being ultimately glorify God. Jesus' kenotic life and death reveal that God engages in self-giving, others-empowering love. To put it differently, Jesus' kenosis reveals that God self-gives to promote overall well-being.[20] The Philippians passage concludes by indicating that God's kenotic love empowers us to promote good as we live out our salvation.[21]

Essential Kenosis and the Primacy of Love

Having clarified what we might mean by *kenōsis*, we need to explore the *essential* in essential kenosis. Essential kenosis considers the self-giving, others-empowering love of God revealed in Jesus Christ to be logically primary in God's eternal essence. In God, love comes first.

---

[20]Some distinguish between *kenōsis* and *plērōsis*. The latter word expresses the fullness of giving, while some interpret *kenōsis* in terms of withdrawing. My understanding of *kenōsis* as self-giving, others-empowering love overcomes the need to complement *kenōsis* with *plērōsis*.
[21]Jeffery F. Keuss explores some dimensions of this in *Freedom of the Self: Kenosis, Cultural Identity, and Mission at the Crossroads* (Eugene, OR: Pickwick, 2010).

Essential kenosis says God's love is a necessary and eternal attribute of God's nature. "[God's] steadfast love endures forever," as the psalmist puts it (throughout Ps 136), because God's loving nature is eternal.

To say kenosis is a necessary, eternal and logically primary attribute of the divine nature means that God expresses kenosis inevitably. Doing so is part of what it means to be God. John's three-word sentence, "God is love" (1 Jn 4:8, 16), can be easily interpreted as supporting this view. "God is love" means love is the necessary expression of God's timeless nature. God relentlessly expresses love in the quest to promote overall well-being (*shalom*).

God must love. To put it as a double negative: God cannot not love. Kenotic love is an essential attribute of God's eternal nature.[22] God loves necessarily. The love creatures express is sporadic, occasional and contingent because creatures do not have eternally loving natures. But God's eternal nature is love, which means God could no more stop loving than stop existing. God's love is uncontrollable, not only in the sense that creatures cannot control divine love but also in the sense that God cannot stop loving. To use a phrase popular among some believers, love is the "heart of God."

Because God must act like God, God must love.

This brings up an important point about the relation between God's love and freedom. God is not free to choose *whether* to love because God's nature is love. Essential kenosis agrees with Jacob Arminius when he says, "God is not freely good; that is, he is not good by the mode of liberty, but by that of natural necessity." For "if God be freely good, he can be or can be made not good." In fact, Arminius considered blasphemous the idea that God is freely good.[23] Similarly, essential kenosis says God's loving goodness is a necessary aspect of God's unchanging nature. It is impossible for God to be unloving because being so would require God to be other than divine.

---

[22]Frank Macchia makes a similar point in *Baptized in the Spirit: A Global Pentecostal Theology* (Grand Rapids: Zondervan, 2006), p. 259.

[23]Jacob Arminius, "It is the Summit of Blasphemy to Say That God Is Freely Good," in *The Works of James Arminius*, trans. James Nichols (1828; repr., Grand Rapids: Baker Books, 1991), 2:33-34.

Essential kenosis says, however, that God freely chooses *how* to express love in each moment. God is free in this important sense. In each moment God freely chooses to love one way instead of another because multiple options are available. God is free when choosing among possible ways to promote *shalom*.

A significant virtue of open and relational theology is that says God loves necessarily. But because it affirms an open future the actual events of which God cannot know until they occur, it also says God freely chooses how to love among various possible loving actions.[24] A God who necessarily loved and foreknew a completed future could not act freely. Although "the steadfast love of the LORD never ceases," it is freely "new every morning" (Lam 3:22-23)!

God necessarily loves, but God freely chooses *how* to love in each emerging moment.

We creatures differ from God in many respects, and Christians have believed it important to stress these differences. Although created in God's image, we are not divine. We can avoid idolatry, in part, by emphasizing God's unique status as the One worthy of our worship. God is God, and creation is not.

Creation differs from God in that free creatures are free both in deciding whether to love and in deciding how to express love. They do not have eternal natures in which love is preeminent and necessary. Because of this, for instance, creatures can choose sin and do evil. God's nature is love, however. This means God can neither sin nor do evil. But God can both want to love us and love us necessarily because love is essential.[25]

Love is God's preeminent attribute. God's kenotic love logically precedes divine power in the divine nature. This logical priority qual-

---

[24]This argument is crucial for overcoming the legitimate criticism William L. Rowe makes against non-open and relational theologies in which a good God necessarily creates the best of all possible worlds. See Rowe's argument in *Can God Be Free?* (Oxford: Oxford University Press, 2004).

[25]I am grateful to Nicholas Carpenter for his discussion that led me to realize that God loving necessarily does not exclude God wanting to love others. Because God's nature is love, God can both want to love creatures and necessarily love them.

ifies how we should think God works in and with creation. As John Wesley puts it, love is God's "reigning attribute,"[26] because as his brother, Charles, sang, "God's name and nature is love."[27] We should agree with C. H. Dodd: "to say 'God is love' implies that *all* His activity is loving activity. If He creates, He creates in love; if He rules, He rules in love; if He judges, He judges in love. All that he does is the expression of his nature, which is—to love."[28] God's attributes—especially power—are best understood in the light of love.

To say love is logically paramount in God does not mean that we disregard other divine attributes, such as sovereignty, omniscience, everlastingness or omnipresence. Nor should we consider the other attributes unimportant. But the way we talk about God reveals how we explicitly or implicitly prioritize these attributes. We saw evidence of this in the previous chapter when various statements from John Sanders reveal that he implicitly affirms God's sovereign choice as logically prior to love.

The vast majority of theologians, in fact, fail to take uncontrolling love as God's logically preeminent attribute. We see the logical prioritizing of sovereign choice, for instance, when theologians say God is free to choose whether to love. Choosing whether to love implies that choice logically comes first for God. If divine love logically precedes divine choice, God necessarily loves because loves comes first. Essential kenosis is exceptional when it says uncontrolling love is logically preeminent in God's nature.

Essential kenosis says love comes first in God.

Essential kenosis stands between two related views of God's love and power. One view says God voluntarily self-limits. God could control others entirely but (usually) chooses not to do so. As we have seen, the voluntary-self-limitation view cannot answer well why God does not un-self-limit, in the name of love, to prevent genuine evil.

---

[26]John Wesley, *Explanatory Notes upon the New Testament* (Salem, OH: Schmul, 1975), p. 637.
[27]Charles Wesley, "Wrestling Jacob," in *A Collection of Hymns for the Use of the People Called Methodists*, vol. 7 of *The Works of John Wesley* (Nashville: Abingdon, 1983), pp. 250-52.
[28]C. H. Dodd, *The Johannine Epistles* (London: Hodder & Stoughton, 1946), p. 112.

But there are other problems with this view.

The voluntary-self-limitation view also implies that love is *not* the logically primary aspect of God's nature. Consequently, the view faces additional problems. If love is not the logically primary attribute, we have no reason to believe that God does not sometimes choose to hate us. If sovereign choice precedes self-giving love, we have no reason to think that God will not sin. If God's nature is not first and foremost love, nothing prevents deity from choosing to break bad. Numerous problems arise when we believe divine will logically comes prior to divine love. Most theologians appeal to mystery when faced with these problems.

We can only trust unreservedly the God in whose nature love is essential, eternal and logically primary.

The other view standing near essential kenosis says external forces or worlds essentially limit God. This view gives the impression that outside actors and powers not of God's making hinder divine power. Or it says God is subject to laws of nature, imposed upon God from without. God is caught in the clutches of exterior authorities and dominions, and these superpowers restrict sovereignty.

This view seems to describe God as a helpless victim to external realities. Some criticize this view as presenting a "finite God" because outside forces or imposed laws curb divine activity. Many wonder how this God can be worthy of worship. While I think we have good reasons to think God's power is limited in certain respects, this view places God under a foreign authority. This God is too small.[29]

Essential kenosis stands between these two views. It rejects both voluntary self-limitation of God and the view that external powers, gods, worlds or laws limit God. Essential kenosis says limitations to divine power derive from God's nature of love. The Creator does not volun-

[29]One of the better books on the quest to find a right-size God is John B. Cobb Jr. and Clark H. Pinnock, eds., *Searching for an Adequate God: A Dialogue Between Process and Free Will Theists* (Grand Rapids: Eerdmans, 2000). Essayists and respondents include David Ray Griffin, William Hasker, Nancy Howell, Richard Rice and David L. Wheeler.

tarily self-limit, nor does creation rule its Maker. Instead, God's self-giving, uncontrolling love is a necessary, eternal and logically primary aspect of the divine nature. And God's actions originate in love.

God's expressions of love takes many forms.[30] Divine love is full-orbed, and Scripture tells us this in various ways. For instance, God expresses *agapē* by repaying evil with good and doing good even to those who act unjustly. *Agapē* promotes *shalom* in response to that which promotes sin, evil and the demonic. God forgives and loves even those who disobey. As our "Father in heaven," God lovingly sends good gifts of sun and rain to all, even to the unjust (Mt 5:45). *Agapē* loves in spite of others who do not love. We should imitate God's *agapē* by turning the other cheek (Mt 5:39) and responding to curses with blessings (Lk 6:28).

God expresses *philia* by partnering with all creation, but especially the more complex creatures, to promote the common good. God is a friend who suffers with us and "daily bears us up" (Ps 68:19). *Philia* promotes well-being by coming alongside to establish collaborative friendships. We can be God's partners and co-conspirators by following the Spirit's lead. God's collaborative love seeks all who want to work for well-being, which is God's purpose (Rom 8:28). In love, God calls us to be "fellow workers" and "co-laborers" (1 Cor 3:9; 2 Cor 6:1).

God expresses *eros* by inspiring and appreciating the beauty of creation and calling creatures to enhance or increase it.[31] God creates the world and calls it "good" (Gen 1:4, 10), and this good creating continues. Despite the evil that sometimes occurs in that world, God continues to appreciate and create beautiful things from the dust. Divine *eros* creates and enhances good in others. We should express *eros* not only by thinking on what is true, honorable, pleasing and excellent; we should express *eros* by doing these things (Phil 4:8-9). The Spirit works in wild

---

[30]See argument for the diversity of forms of love in Daniel Day Williams, *The Spirit and the Forms of Love* (New York: Harper & Row, 1968); and Nicholas Wolterstorff, *Justice in Love* (Grand Rapids: Eerdmans, 2011), chap. 9.

[31]Elaine Padilla argues this forcefully in *Divine Enjoyment: A Theology of Passion and Exuberance* (New York: Fordham University Press, 2015).

and wonderful ways to love a world created good.

God promotes overall well-being through full-orbed love.

Divine love gives and receives, empowering creatures to live, live better and live well. God takes into account the context and relationships of each creature when acting for its good. This involves God offering forms of life, possibilities, opportunities and various other ways of existing. While God always loves to the utmost, the forms of divine love vary depending on the situation, entity or creature. God is intimately involved, and divine love is pluriform.

Loving diverse others requires diverse actions from deity. God is not a steady-state force or impersonal iceberg. Instead, essential kenosis affirms that divine action varies because God is personally involved in giving and receiving relations with all creatures. The heavenly vision for well-being prompts diverse divine actions of love. While God's love is unwavering and wholehearted, the way God loves varies from moment to moment, creature to creature.[32] Only a personal God loves in such reciprocal relationships.

Divine love is tailor-made for each creature in each instant.

In all of this, God seeks *shalom*, also known as the kingdom of God. Because God loves the world (Jn 3:16) and desires to redeem all creation (Rom 8:19-22), all creatures are recipients of divine love. God acts variously to establish the reign of love throughout all creation as the Great Lover of us all. This work of love involves promoting overall well-being in its widely diverse and multiple dimensions.[33] God's providence promotes the ways and power of love. The love of God is shed abroad because the Spirit cares about each creature and the common good (Rom 5:5). Abundant is the love God lavishes upon creation (1 Jn 3:1)!

---

[32]I explore this set of ideas in "Testing Creaturely Love and God's Causal Role," in *The Science and Theology of Godly Love*, ed. Matthew T. Lee and Amos Yong (DeKalb: Northern Illinois University Press, 2012), pp. 94-120.

[33]I address the dominant forms of love, including defining these forms, in *Defining Love: A Philosophical, Scientific, and Theological Engagement* (Grand Rapids: Brazos, 2010), chaps. 2, 6; and throughout *The Nature of Love: A Theology* (St. Louis: Chalice, 2010). These books also delve into issues of divine love and the meaning of well-being.

ESSENTIAL KENOSIS AND EVIL

The preceding sets the stage for explaining how essential kenosis answers the primary question thwarting efforts to make sense of life: why doesn't a loving and powerful God prevent genuine evil? The essential kenosis model of providence offers one principal answer, although it includes various dimensions. Let me state this answer simply:

God *cannot* unilaterally prevent genuine evil.

For some people, to say "God cannot" is to blaspheme. In their view, God's power has no limits whatsoever. Those who embrace the omni-cause model of providence, for instance, cringe when they hear the phrase "God cannot." They will not reconsider their belief that God controls all things, even in light of God's self-giving, others-empowering love. To them, God's sovereignty requires unlimited omnipotence.

Most theologians and theistic philosophers throughout history, however, have said we cannot understand God's power well if we believe it unconditionally unlimited. God cannot bring about all conceivable states of affairs.[34] There are limits to God's power.

Most scholars say, for instance, that God cannot do what is illogical. God cannot make a round square, cannot make 2 + 2 = 5 and cannot simultaneously make a man both married and a bachelor. God cannot make us free and not free at the same time.[35] These activities would require God to do what is logically contradictory, and as Thomas Aquinas says, "whatever involves a contradiction is not within the scope of [God's] omnipotence."[36]

Most Christian scholars say God cannot do other things. God cannot change the past, for instance. God cannot now make Martha Washington the first president of the United States because George was actually first. God cannot now prevent the Nazi holocaust because

---

[34]For a concise summary of the issues of God's limitations in relation to omnipotence, see Joshua Hoffman and Gary Rosenkrantz, "Omnipotence," in *A Companion to Philosophy of Religion*, ed. Philip L. Quinn and Charles Taliaferro (Malden, MA: Blackwell, 1999), pp. 229-35.

[35]One of the more influential defenses in response to charges that theism is logically incompatible with evil is Alvin Plantinga's work in *God, Freedom, and Evil* (Grand Rapids: Eerdmans, 1977).

[36]Thomas Aquinas, *Summa Theologica* (New York: McGraw-Hill, 1963), 1.15.3, pp. 163-64.

those days are (thankfully!) over. God cannot change the outcome of Super Bowl XLII to give the New England Patriots a perfect season.

The belief that God cannot change the past arises from the commonsense view that backward causation is impossible. Aquinas is again helpful: "Some things . . . at one time were in the nature of possibility . . . [but] now fall short of the nature of possibility." Consequently, "God is not able to do them, because they themselves cannot be done."[37] Reverse causation is impossible even for God.

Many scholars also say God cannot act contrary to God's own nature. "[God] cannot deny himself," as Paul puts it (2 Tim 2:13), or change the divine essence, as James says (Jas 1:17). Scripture mentions other things God cannot do because of God's unchanging nature. For instance, God cannot lie (Heb 6:18; Tit 1:2), cannot be tempted by evil (Jas 1:12) and cannot become exhausted (Is 40:28). The Bible explicitly says God cannot do some things.

Most scholars also say God cannot do other things.[38] For instance, God cannot decide to be 467 parts instead of triune, cannot sin, cannot self-duplicate and cannot self-annihilate. These limitations derive from God's own nature, not from some outside force or factor. "When we make such assertions as these," says Jacob Arminius, "we do not inflict an injury on the capability of God." We must beware, says Arminius, "that things unworthy of Him not be attributed to his essence, his understanding, and his will."[39] As C. S. Lewis puts it, "not even Omnipotence can do what is self-contradictory."[40] God cannot do some things because they are inherently impossible for deity.

Absolute sovereignty is absolutely unbelievable.

---

[37]Thomas Aquinas, *Summa Theologica* (New York: Cosmo, 2007), 1.25.4, p. 139. Jonathan Edwards puts it this way: "In explaining the nature of necessity, that in things which are past, their past existence is now necessary" (*Freedom of the Will*, [New York: Leavitt & Allen, 1857], p. 10, §12). See also Alvin Plantinga, "On Ockham's Way Out," *Faith and Philosophy* 3 (July 1986): 235-69. I am grateful to James Goetz and Frank Macchia for alerting me to some of this material.

[38]Jacob Arminius offers a long list of things God cannot do in "Twenty-Five Public Disputations," in *The Works of James Arminius*, trans. James Nichols (1828; repr., Grand Rapids: Baker Books, 1991), 1:135.

[39]Ibid.

[40]C. S. Lewis, *Miracles: A Preliminary Study* (New York: HarperCollins, 2001), p. 90.

Essential kenosis endorses these limitations on God's power. But it adds an important limitation to the list by identifying another set of actions not possible for God. This additional set of actions is not possible because uncontrolling love is the logically preeminent attribute of God's nature.

Essential kenosis says God's self-giving, others-empowering nature of love necessarily provides freedom, agency, self-organization and lawlike regularity to creation. Because love is the preeminent and necessary attribute in God's nature, God cannot withdraw, override or fail to provide the freedom, agency, self-organizing and lawlike regularity God gives. Divine love limits divine power.

God cannot deny God's own nature, which necessarily expresses self-giving, others-empowering love.

When giving freedom, agency, self-organization and lawlike regularity to creation, the gifts God gives are, to use the Paul's language, "irrevocable" (Rom 11:29). Out of love, God necessarily gifts others in their moment-by-moment existence, and God cannot rescind these endowments. To do so, says essential kenosis, would require God to deny the divine nature of love. And according to Scripture, that's not possible.

This aspect of divine limitation makes it possible to solve the problem of evil.[41] It also allows essential kenosis to answer other perplexing questions of existence.[42] Essential kenosis explains why God cannot prevent the genuine evil that creatures cause, including

---

[41]My full solution to the problem of evil involves five aspects. I am mainly addressing the theoretical aspect in this book, which revolves around reconceiving divine power. The other aspects pertain to divine empathy, pedagogy, healing and strategic activism. I sketch out those dimensions in my essay "An Essential Kenosis Solution to the Problem of Evil," in *God and the Problem of Evil*, ed. James K. Dew Jr. and Chad Meister (Downers Grove, IL: InterVarsity Press, forthcoming).

[42]For instance, essential kenosis explains why God cannot totally control creatures to provide crystal-clear, unambiguous and therefore inerrant revelation. It also explains why God cannot entirely control situations so that just and equal distribution of goods and services is provided to all. And it can be part of an overall theory of initial creation that avoids the pitfalls of *creatio ex nihilo*. For my thoughts on this latter issue, see "God Always Creates out of Creation in Love: *Creatio ex Creatione a Natura Amoris*," in *Theologies of Creation: Creatio ex Nihilo and Its New Rivals*, ed. Thomas Jay Oord (New York: Routledge, 2014), pp. 109-22.

the genuine evils we encountered when reading the true stories in chapter one. Here are some reasons why:

First, this model of providence says God necessarily gives freedom to all creatures complex enough to receive and express it. Giving freedom is part of God's steadfast love. This means God cannot withdraw, override or fail to provide the freedom a perpetrator of evil expresses. God must give freedom, even to those who use it wrongly.

John Wesley describes this aspect of essential kenosis well. When explaining providence, Wesley says, "Were human liberty taken away, men would be as incapable of virtue as stones. Therefore (with reverence be it spoken) the Almighty himself *cannot* do this thing. He cannot thus contradict himself or undo what he has done."[43] God must give and cannot take away free will.

Essential kenosis applies this to all life. But it especially helps to make sense of intense suffering and atrocities caused by free choices. By acting alone, God cannot thwart evil freely done by those exercising divinely derived freedom. Consequently, this model of providence allows us to say God is not culpable for failing to prevent the dastardly deeds free creatures do.

Because of God's immutable nature of self-giving, others-empowering love, God cannot prevent genuine evil.

For instance, as God immediately became aware of the Tsarnaev brothers' plans, God could predict they would plant bombs alongside the route of the Boston Marathon. But because God necessarily gives freedom, God could not unilaterally prevent the bombing. To do so would require removing free will from the brothers, which a loving God who necessarily gives freedom cannot do. Therefore, God could not have prevented the Boston Marathon bombing by acting alone.

Because God necessarily gave freedom to those who raped Zamuda

[43]John Wesley, "On Divine Providence," sermon 67, in *The Works of John Wesley*, ed. Albert C. Outler (Nashville: Abingdon, 1985), pp. 534-550, § 15. Wesley also says that God does not "take away your liberty, your power of choosing good or evil." He argues that "[God] did not *force* you, but being *assisted* by [God's] grace you, like Mary, *chose* the better part." "The General Spread of the Gospel," sermon 63, in *The Works of John Wesley*, ed. Albert C. Outler (Nashville: Abingdon, 1985), 2:281, emphasis original.

and killed her family, God could not have prevented this tragedy by acting alone. God's love is uncontrolling, and in kenotic love God provides freedom to others, including Zamuda's torturers. Consequently, God is not culpable for failing to prevent Zamuda's pain and the death of her family.

It is important to distinguish between God being influential when giving freedom and God being morally culpable for failing to prevent evil. Essential kenosis affirms God's pervasive influence but denies that God can control others. Because God providentially gives freedom to creatures complex enough to express it, God gives freedom that creatures use for good or evil (or morally neutral) activities. God acts as a necessary, though partial, cause for all creaturely activity.

Because God *must* give freedom and cannot override the gift given, we should not blame God when creatures misuse freedom. An uncontrolling God is not culpable when creatures oppose what this loving God desires. Creatures are blameworthy.

Parenting illustrates this. The parents of a rapist are causally responsible for bringing him into the world. Their sexual union made possible his existence. Assuming these parents did an adequate job of teaching their son right and wrong, we would not consider them morally culpable when their son freely chooses rape. We blame the rapist and regard him as culpable, not his parents, although the parents are necessary causes for his existence.

Analogously, God creates and gives freedom to do good or ill in each moment. But God's self-giving, others-empowering love means God cannot withdraw, fail to provide or override the freedom God necessarily gives. Consequently, we are wrong to blame God when genuine evil occurs. God is not culpable.

God's love necessarily gives freedom.

Second, essential kenosis explains why God doesn't prevent evil that simple creatures with agency cause or even simpler entities with mere self-organizing capacities cause. God necessarily gives the gifts of agency and self-organization to entities capable of them because doing so is part of divine love. God's others-empowering love extends to the least and simplest of these.

God cannot withdraw, override or fail to provide agency and self-organizing to any simple organism or entity that causes genuine evil. The kenotic love of God necessarily provides agency and self-organization. God's moment-by-moment gifts are irrevocable. Consequently, God is not culpable for failing to prevent the evil that basic entities, organisms and simple creatures may cause.

For instance, cellular or genetic mutations and the malfunction of simple structures in baby Eliana Tova apparently caused her debilitating condition. Because God necessarily gives agency and self-organization to the entities and organs of our bodies, God could not unilaterally prevent Eliana Tova's ailments. To prevent them would require God to withdraw, override or fail to provide agency and self-organization to her body's basic organisms, entities and structures. A loving God who necessarily self-gives and others-empowers cannot do this.

Realizing that God cannot unilaterally prevent suffering caused by simple entities helps us make sense of suffering caused by natural malfunctions or disasters. This means, for instance, we should not accuse God of causing or allowing birth defects, cancer, infections, disease, hurricanes, earthquakes, tsunamis, or other illnesses and catastrophes. The degradation brought by such calamities does not represent God's will. Instead, we can blame simple structures, various natural processes of the world, small organisms or creation gone awry. Because God's self-giving, others-empowering love makes agency and self-organization possible, God is not culpable for the evil that less-complex entities cause.

In the previous chapter, we looked briefly at the free-process response to evil. Although I criticized one form of the free-process response, essential kenosis affirms an alternative form. Because essential kenosis says God gives agency and self-organization to creation and this giving derives from God's loving essence, it overcomes problems that arise in versions of the free-process defense that imply God's gifting is entirely voluntary. According to essential kenosis, the dynamic, sometimes chaotic and partially random universe with its various systems and processes emerges from God's necessarily creative and kenotic love. The free process of life is an essential expression of divine grace.

God's love necessarily gives agency and self-organization.

Third, essential kenosis helps us make sense of the random mutations, chance events and accidents that cause evil. While some randomness is beneficial, other randomness is devastating and fails to make the world as good as it could have been. We should not blame anyone or anything for randomly generated misfortunes. They are indiscriminate, unplanned and unforeseen. But essential kenosis explains why God doesn't prevent them.

Preventing evils caused by random events would require God to foreknow and control these events occurring at whatever level of complexity we find them. Controlling randomness would require God to withhold the simple power to become and exist with stable regularity. To control randomness, God would need to foreknow random events were about to occur and then interrupt the lawlike regularities of existence that make them possible. But to do so, says essential kenosis, God would have to "deny himself," to use biblical language. God cannot do this, because the gifts of lawlike regularities are irrevocable, and God does not know which possibilities for randomness will become actual.

God's universal and steadfast self-giving love has the effect of establishing lawlike regularities throughout creation as God lovingly makes existence possible. The spontaneity present at all levels of existence derives from God's gift of existence. Kenotic love necessarily imparts lawlike regularities as God creates and interacts with creatures. The lawlike regularities of the universe derive from God's loving expressions, which themselves are grounded in God's nature of uncontrolling love.

In chapter two, we explored Euthyphro's dilemma in light of lawlike regularities or what many call the "laws of nature." We noted problems with saying that God created these laws. We also noted problems with saying that natural laws are external to God. I briefly offered a third way.

Essential kenosis says that lawlike regularities in creation derive from God's persistent and loving activity. These regularities are neither entirely voluntary nor do they transcend God from the outside. Rather, God's loving activities reflect the eternally unchanging divine essence of love. Consequently, God's loving nature is the ultimate source of creation's lawlike regularities, and the God who loves necessarily cannot interrupt the love expressed to all. Rather than being an external watchmaker, God's ongoing, ever-influential love conditions all creation as the One in whom all things live and move and have their being (Acts 17:28).

Lawlike regularities affect all creation. But they especially regulate the simplest entities and aggregate systems of existence. Simple entities have far less flexibility. Aggregates—like planets, pebbles and paper—are not self-organizing agents. Interrupting lawlike regularities would require God to fail to provide existence to portions of creation. But God cannot do this because of steadfast love.

Regularities of existence—so-called natural laws—emerged in evolutionary history as new kinds of organisms emerged in response to God's love. The consistency of divine love creates regularities as creatures respond, given the nature of their existence and the degree and range of agency they possess. God's eternal nature of love both sets limits and offers possibilities to each creature and context, depending on their complexity. In this, God's love orders the world. And because God's nature is love, God cannot override the order that emerges.

On this issue, I agree with John Polkinghorne when he says that "the regularities of the mechanical aspects of nature are to be understood theologically as signs of the faithfulness of the Creator."[44] Essential kenosis adds, however, that the Creator's faithfulness derives from that Creator's loving nature. In fact, it is in the context of the apostle Paul emphasizing divine faithfulness that we find the biblical

---

[44]In Thomas Jay Oord, ed., *The Polkinghorne Reader: Science, Faith and the Search for Meaning* (Philadelphia: Templeton Press, 2010), pp. 124-25.

claim about God's inherent limitations: "[God] remains faithful," because God "cannot deny himself" (2 Tim 2:13).

Polkinghorne also says that the regularities described by physics "are pale reflections of [God's] faithfulness towards his creation. . . . He will not interfere in their operation in a fitful or capricious way, for that would be for the Eternally Reliable to turn himself into an occasional conjurer."[45] I agree with Polkinghorne here as well. But I would say that God *cannot* interfere with these lawlike regularities, not just that God *will not* interfere.

The processes and regularities in life derive from God's nature of essentially kenotic love.

For instance, God could not have unilaterally prevented the rock that killed the Canadian woman whose story we encountered earlier. Because God necessarily gives existence to all creation—including rocks—and because existence is characterized by lawlike regularities, God alone could not have averted this tragedy. To prevent unilaterally the rock killing the woman, God would need to forgo loving interaction with some portion of creation. Contradicting God's nature and thereby failing to love creation—even failing to love rocks by not endowing them with existence—is something a necessarily loving God cannot do.[46]

Additionally, God could not have foreknown this specific accident. Although God would have known it was possible, various random factors and the free will of both drivers mitigate against God's foreknowing that an errant rock would cause this tragic death. God's ongoing presence in all moments of time is *time-full*. Essential kenosis takes the time-full reality of existence and God's time-full existing as crucial for understanding why God cannot foreknow or prevent genuine evils such as this. Divine love necessarily compels God to act in ways that generate lawlike regularity.

---

[45]John C. Polkinghorne, *Science and Providence: God's Interaction with the World* (West Conshohocken, PA: Templeton Press, 2005), p. 30.

[46]For one of the better explorations of God's love and power in relation to all of creation, especially nonhumans, see Christopher Southgate, *The Groaning of Creation: God, Evolution, and the Problem of Evil* (Louisville, KY: Westminster John Knox, 2008).

God Is an Omnipresent Spirit

While we should say God cannot prevent genuine evil because doing so requires nullifying the divine nature of uncontrolling love, another important set of issues remains. These issues are part of fundamental claim of essential kenosis that God acting alone cannot prevent genuine evil. Let me begin to address these issues with this question: if we creatures sometimes thwart a planned terrorist attack or some other act of evil, why can't a loving God?

For instance, if we can step between two combatants intent on throwing punches and thereby prevent evil, why can't God do the same? If parents can sometimes stop one child from injuring another, why can't God? If we can build a dam and thereby stop a flash flood from wreaking unnecessary havoc, why can't God prevent evil this way? And if creatures can marshal others to use tools or instruments to prevent genuine evil, why doesn't God do the same? We don't need foreknowledge to prevent such evils. Why can't a God without exhaustive foreknowledge do what we sometimes can?

To answer these questions, we need to look at a fourth way that essential kenosis says God is limited. This answer affirms the traditional Christian view that God is a loving, omnipresent spirit. Those who affirm this traditional view, however, often fail to think through its implications. Believing God is an omnipresent spirit has consequences for answering well why God cannot prevent evil in ways we sometimes might.

Being an omnipresent spirit affords God unique abilities and limitations.

To say God is a loving spirit is to say, in part, that God does not have a divine body. God's essential "being" or "constitution" is spiritual. The classic language is "incorporeal." Jesus says, "God is spirit" (Jn 4:24), and Scripture is replete with similar statements about God's being. Essential kenosis affirms the common Christian view that God is essentially an incorporeal and omnipresent agent.

Because God is spirit, we cannot perceive God directly with our five senses. We cannot literally taste, touch, see, hear or smell God.

Christians have proposed various theories, however, to explain how God's spiritual presence exerts causal force upon creation.[47] The details of these theories deserve a fuller explanation than possible here.[48] But I am attracted to theories that conceive of God as a spirit whom we *directly* perceive through nonsensory means.[49] I also believe we can infer God's actions indirectly by perceiving what God has made, including the created world in general, other creatures and ourselves.

The second divine attribute typically neglected in discussions of evil is God's universality. God is present to all creation and to each entity because God is omnipresent. Rather than being localized in a particular place in the way creatures are localized, the Creator is present to all.

To say that God is an omnipresent spirit does not need to mean that God has no physicality whatsoever. I believe there is always a physical dimension to the divine presence although we cannot perceive it with our five senses. Describing God's omnipresence and physicality in God has always been difficult for Christians because God is not locally situated and not perceptible by our five senses.

Attempts to describe the Creator using creaturely comparisons are partly helpful. There is a venerable tradition within Christian theology, for instance, that says God is like a mind. The Hebrew word *ruakh* sometimes refers to God and can be translated "mind." This analogy is helpful because although we cannot perceive minds with our five senses, we believe they have causal influence. Minds also have a subjective unity, which allows them to make decisions and act purposively. God's spiritual being is like a mind in these ways.

Saying God is like a mind, however, has several weaknesses. For instance, creaturely minds are not omnipresent whereas God is om-

---

[47]See Thomas Jay Oord, "The Divine Spirit as Causal and Personal," *Zygon* 48, no. 2 (2013): 466-77.

[48]I propose one solution in Thomas Jay Oord, "A Postmodern Wesleyan Philosophy and David Ray Griffin's Postmodern Vision," *Wesleyan Theological Journal* 35, no. 1 (2000): 216-44.

[49]I have been influenced toward this view by theologians like John B. Cobb Jr., who speaks of "nonsensory perception of God" and "nonsensuous experience of the divine presence in our lives" (*Grace and Responsibility: A Wesleyan Theology for Today* [Nashville: Abingdon, 1995], p. 75). But other theologians propose theories to account for divine causation by the Spirit.

nipresent. Creaturely minds, say most people, have a beginning. By contrast, God is everlasting. And depending on what mind-body theory one affirms, we may wonder if the mind has a physical dimension, although I think it does.

I particularly like the analogy that says God's spiritual being is like air or wind. This description appears many places in Scripture. In fact, the New Testament word for "spirit"—*pneuma*—is also the word for "wind" or "air." And the biblical word *ruakh* can be translated "breath." Wind has a physical dimension although we cannot see it. Wind also exerts causal force. We see the effects of the wind, sometimes by observing tiny particles as they are whisked about.

Just as we cannot see wind, we also cannot see God. Despite not being observed, we attribute at least some effects in our world to divine causation (Jn 3:8). Many of us believe ourselves influenced by this unseen Friend, for instance. And some biblical passages suggest that air—breath—is God's creating presence. As Job puts it,

The spirit of God has made me,
    and the breath of the Almighty gives me life. (Job 33:4)

The wind analogy also has limitations, of course. Wind is not omnipresent, which means it can flow, move from one place to another and be absent in some things. Air also has no will so it cannot make decisions or act purposively. Wind possesses no subjective experience.

All analogies between God's spiritual being and something creaturely fail in some way. My main point in exploring God's being as a loving omnipresent spirit, however, is to help us think about why God cannot by using a divine body to prevent genuine evil.

As an omnipresent spirit with no localized divine body, God cannot exert divine bodily influence as a localized corpus. This means God cannot use a divine body to step between two parties engaged in a fight, for instance. God doesn't have a wholly divine hand to scoop a rock out of the air, cover a bomb before it explodes or block a bullet before it projects from a rifle. While we may sometimes be blameworthy for failing to use our bodies to prevent genuine evils, the God without a localized divine body is not culpable.

God cannot prevent evil with a localized divine body because God is an omnipresent spirit.[50]

God can, however, marshal through persuasion those with localized bodies. They can exert creaturely bodily impact in various ways. God can call a teacher to stand between a bully and the bully's victim. God can call the firefighter to reach through a burning window to grab a terrified toddler. God can even call lesser organisms and entities to use their bodily aspects, in whatever limited way, to promote good or prevent evil. In all this, says essential kenosis, God acts without having a localized divine body and without totally controlling others.

Of course, creatures and organisms may not respond well to God's call. God may want to prevent some evil and call a creature to use its body for that purpose. But creatures may fail to respond well, disobey and sin. Humans above all other creatures know well the reality of using their bodies for evil ends. Most believers call this sin.

The omnipresent Spirit is not culpable for the evil that results when creatures fail to love. God may want groups to intercede, but these groups may ignore God's commands. When we fail to respond well to God calls, we are to blame. The loving and omnipresent Spirit without a localized divine body is not guilty.

Thankfully, creatures sometimes respond well to God's call. They "listen" to God's call to prevent some impending tragedy or stop an ongoing conflict. When creatures respond well, we might even say that God prevented that evil. This should not mean that God *alone* prevented it. Creatures cooperated, playing necessary roles by using their bodies to fulfill God's good purposes. Our saying God did it should be interpreted as expressing the belief that God played the primary causal role in the event or is the ultimate source of this positive activity.

---

[50]Depending on one's view of the incarnation, of course, one may think Jesus is an exception to the view that God does not have a localized divine body. That discussion requires another book. But I agree with many theologians who distinguish between God's essential and eternal being and God's temporary incarnation as a localized human, Jesus of Nazareth.

Creaturely cooperation inspired the statement "we are God's hands and feet." It also inspired the saying "the world is God's body" because we can act as members of the body of Christ (1 Cor 12:15-19). These statements only make sense, however, if we do not take them literally. We do not literally become divine appendages; the world is not literally a divine corpus. God remains divine, and we are God's creations.

When creatures respond well to God's leading, the overall result is that God's will is done "on earth as it is in heaven." When God's loving will is done, we might credit, praise and thank the Creator. "Thanks be to God!" This oft-spoken phrase is appropriate. But we can also rightly acknowledge creaturely cooperation required for establishing what is good. Creatures can be God's co-workers, ambassadors and viceroys.[51] God gets the lion's share of the credit for good, but it is also appropriate to thank creatures who cooperate with their Creator. A thankful pat on a neighbor's back does not rob God of glory.

A Coercive God of Love Is Fictional

In the previous chapter, I said the God whose preeminent attribute is uncontrolling love could not create controllable creatures. If God's love cooperates rather than controls, never forces its way on the beloved and risks rather than imposes guarantees, love as the logically preeminent attribute prevents God from entirely determining others. An essentially loving God who *could* totally control others does not exist because God's love cannot control. To illustrate my argument, I said the idea that a loving God could control others is as fictional as the idea that mermaids could run marathons.

Essential kenosis explains why the God whose logically preeminent attribute is love cannot control others. If God were to coerce others by withdrawing, overriding or failing to provide freedom, agency or self-organization, God would need to renounce the divine nature of self-giving, others-empowering love. If God were to

---

[51]For the biblical justification of this view, see 1 Cor 3:9; 2 Cor 5:20; 6:1; Eph 6:11-12; 2 Tim 2:3-4, 12; Rev 5:10; 20:6; 22:5.

prevent random events by interrupting the lawlike regularities of existence, God would need to renounce the divine nature of uncontrolling love. But God cannot contradict God's own nature, so divine coercion is impossible.

In light of essential kenosis, we might rephrase the mermaid illustration: the idea that God, whose logically preeminent attribute is self-giving, others-empowering love, could override, fail to provide or withdraw freedom, agency or self-organization or could interrupt the lawlike regularities of existence is as fictional as the idea that mermaids could run marathons. Mermaids cannot run marathons, and a kenotic God cannot coerce.

A controlling God of love is fictional.

A number of people take it as obvious that, as John Sanders put it, "love does not force its own way on the beloved."[52] They agree with Sanders when he says God's love "does not force [creatures] to comply."[53] In these statements, Sanders expresses the common view that love never coerces, in the sense of controlling others entirely or forcing its own way. To people with this view, it is a fundamental given—an a priori truth—that love does not withdraw, override or fail to support the freedom, agency or self-organization of others. Love does not control.

Let's call this common view "love by definition is noncoercive." This view arises from the deep intuition that love never controls others entirely. In relation to the God whose nature is love, this view entails that God *cannot* control others entirely. If love is inherently uncontrolling and God loves necessarily, God is incapable of coercion.

The claim that God cannot coerce, however, is especially vulnerable to misunderstanding. *Coerce* has multiple meanings. In everyday language, we often use the word in its psychological sense. In this sense, to coerce is to place intense psychological pressure on a creature or group to motivate it to act in a particular manner. To those being

---

[52]John Sanders, *The God Who Risks: A Theology of Providence*, rev. ed. (Downers Grove, IL: InterVarsity Press, 2007), p. 193.
[53]Ibid., p. 174.

pressured, this may feel like bullying, a serious threat or extreme force.

In the psychological sense of *coerce*, the person being coerced retains free will. Threats and emotional pressures do not deprive their subjects of freedom. The person may yield to the pressure and thereby avoid negative consequences or gain positive ones. The person may freely choose not to yield and thereby reap negative consequences. Coercion, in the psychological sense, doesn't entail total control of others because those involved retain some measure of free will.

Others equate the word *coerce* with violence. Those wanting to reduce violence in the world (which includes most people) may say they want to reduce coercion. Actions that these people label as coercive include violent acts of war, domestic altercations, interpersonal conflict and acts of terror. For them, to act violently is to coerce. In such cases, violence involves bodies or other localized physical objects wreaking destruction.

A growing literature explores whether it makes sense to say God is violent or ever calls us to use our bodies or other objects violently.[54] Some in this discussion also use *coerce* to mean "act violently." Often at the center of this debate is how to interpret particular scriptural passages suggesting divine violence and the apparently violent actions of Jesus. Sometimes the question is whether we ought to use violent force when acting in relation to others.

A third way some use *coerce* pertains to the use of bodies to impact other bodies. The parent who picks up a screaming two-year-old and puts the child in a crib may be said to coerce or control the two-year-old. The child may not want to be in the crib. But the stronger and bigger body prevails. We might call this the bodily impact sense of *coerce*, because it involves bodies exerting force upon other bodies and things in the world.

I am not using *coerce* in the psychological, violence or bodily impact senses. I am using it in the metaphysical sense. In the meta-

---

[54]The number of important books on this subject is large. One of the better contributions is Eric A. Seibert, *The Violence of Scripture: Overcoming the Old Testament's Troubling Legacy* (Philadelphia: Fortress, 2012).

physical sense, to coerce is to control entirely. This involves unilateral determination, in which the one coerced loses all capacity for causation, self-organization, agency or free will. To coerce in this metaphysical sense is to act as a sufficient cause, thereby wholly controlling the other or the situation. To coerce is to control.

Love does not coerce in the metaphysical sense because it never controls others. Applied to God, the inability to coerce in the metaphysical sense means God cannot control others or situations. God's love is uncontrolling.[55] Essential kenosis says God cannot coerce, in the sense of acting as a sufficient cause or unilaterally determining others. In addition, God is not a bully and God does not act violently. Because God does not have a localized physical body with which to exert direct bodily impact, God does not use divine bodily impact.[56]

Divine love is uncontrolling, which means God cannot coerce.

Some people, however, are not convinced that love *never* forces its way or controls others. They admit love usually invites cooperation or contribution. They may think love typically does not overrule or overpower. But they think love might at times require coercion in the metaphysical sense. Therefore, they think God sometimes coerces.

These people can imagine instances in which, if it were possible, a loving person ought to control another person or situation to guarantee a positive outcome or avoid an evil one. For them, love is *not* by definition uncontrolling. When it comes to God, these people believe divine love sometimes involves coercion, in the metaphysical sense of completely controlling others or situations.

To those unconvinced that love, a priori, never forces its way, a robust a posteriori argument exists for why God's love never coerces. In other words, there is compelling evidence for why we should think

---

[55]Catherine Keller endorses this view in *God and Power: Counter-Apocalyptic Journeys* (Minneapolis: Fortress, 2005).

[56]Essential kenosis is neutral on whether God ever calls creatures to act violently. There are good reasons, however, to interpret biblical texts, broadly speaking, as advocating nonviolence. On this, see C. S. Cowles, *Show Them No Mercy: Four Views on God and Canaanite Genocide* (Grand Rapids: Zondervan, 2003); Gregory Love, *Love, Violence, and the Cross: How the Nonviolent God Saves Us Through the Cross of Christ* (Eugene, OR: Cascade, 2010); and Seibert, *Violence of Scripture*.

God cannot control others entirely. Using abductive argument, it makes sense to say God cannot coerce based on this evidence. In short, the evidence suggests God cannot coerce.

Few explore this view adequately. Perhaps those who know it are reticent to rethink their assumptions about God's power. Many may not feel comfortable thinking God has limitations, even if those limitations originate from God's nature. Some may believe reconceiving God's power opposes traditional theological views. Some may worry about political or social implications should they rethink their view of God's power.

The idea that the evidence suggests God cannot coerce begins with a common view of divine love. It says the God who loves perfectly would want to prevent all genuine evil. God's care would entail thwarting horrors and tragedies if doing so were possible. Many believers affirm this way of thinking about divine benevolence. To many, in fact, "perfect love" (1 Jn 4:18) seems to require it. God would want to prevent every event that, all things considered, makes the world worse than it might have been had another possible event occurred instead.

The argument from evidence affirms that God seeks to establish the kingdom of love, to use biblical language. Among other things, this means promoting overall well-being, flourishing or *shalom*. Our loving Heavenly Parent, like loving earthly parents, wants to promote good and prevent genuine evil because God abhors evil and desires the common good. God cares for all.

Jesus Christ is primary evidence for most Christians that God seeks well-being through noncoercive means. Although Jesus can be angry or even exert strong force on occasion (e.g., clearing the temple), Jesus never acted coercively in the sense of controlling others entirely. The a posteriori evidence of the life of Jesus, whom Christians believe reveals God better than any other person, suggests that God does not coerce.

The argument from evidence also affirms that genuinely evil events occur. Evil is real. Our fundamental intuitions tell us that some events make the world worse overall, and at least some such events could have been avoided. Genuine evils need not have occurred. We encountered examples of genuine evils in chapter one. But we could point to countless others.

We not only find evidence for genuine evil in what we encounter; we also act as if genuine evil occurs. As we saw in earlier discussions, this is one of life's experiential nonnegotiables. Our natural reactions demonstrate that we know evil happens, even if some people deny it in what they say or write. The way we live our lives reflects our fundamental intuition that genuinely evil events occur.

Upon affirming that a loving God wants to prevent genuine evil though genuine evils occur, the argument from evidence concludes that a loving God must not prevent genuine evil because God cannot control others or situations. In other words, the evidence indicates or suggests that God cannot coerce. To put it differently: because genuine evils occur and God always loves, we are right to infer that God must not be able to coerce to prevent genuine evil. This abductive argument is straightforward. But preconceived notions of God's power often prevent many from taking it seriously.

The argument from evidence, of course, is susceptible to counterarguments. Reasoning from evidence is never airtight, and abduction involves interpretation. In previous chapters, we explored some of those counterarguments, but none proved convincing.[57]

There is one counterargument to the claim that the evidence of life suggests God cannot coerce, however, that I find more robust. Rather than appealing to mystery, this argument says we *do* have evidence that God sometimes coerces, in the metaphysical sense of the word. Sometimes God *does* control others or situations. In other words, this argument also appeals to evidence.

---

[57]The main counterargument given for why a God of love would not prevent genuine evil is not really an argument at all. It's an appeal to mystery. Implicitly or explicitly, many say we cannot know whether the events we consider genuinely evil actually are so. Many people say God has some immediate reason or future plan that requires suffering. In some mysterious way, God preventing suffering would be worse than allowing it. Mystery appeals cannot provide satisfying answers to our most fundamental questions, especially those related to God's providence in light of good and evil, randomness and regularity. The mystery card spoils the deck.

Those who say God sometimes controls entirely point to unusual, astonishing or baffling events that are good. They claim God entirely controlled the situation or individuals required to make these events possible. In fact, this is how some people define a miracle: a supernatural act in which God totally controls an individual or situation or interrupts natural causes to bring about an unusual but positive outcome.

Those who make this argument often point to miracles in the Bible or their own lives. Such miracles may involve healings, serendipities, exorcisms, transformed lives or even resurrections. They claim these unusual events provide evidence that God sometimes controls others or situations. In their view, God would have to coerce for these events to occur.

I think this argument is worth exploring. After all, I also believe in miracles. I think an adequate model of divine providence needs to account for miracles—miracles in Scripture and those we encounter today—if it can make sense of life. Miracles matter.

I believe we can affirm miracles we consider authentic, however, without also claiming God controls others entirely or interrupts natural laws. To explain my view, I explore miracles in the final chapter. My exploration accounts for miracles in light of essential kenosis. I believe that an all-loving and almighty God acts providentially and sometimes miraculously through self-giving, others-empowering love. But this never involves control because God's love is uncontrolling.

For the remainder of this book, visit your favorite bookseller...

THOMAS
JAY OORD

The
Uncontrolling
Love *of* God

AN OPEN AND RELATIONAL
ACCOUNT OF PROVIDENCE

Pluriform Love

AN OPEN AND RELATIONAL
THEOLOGY OF WELL-BEING

Table of Contents

9

A Theology of Pluriform Love

THE PRIMACY AND MEANING OF LOVE

A theology of pluriform love makes sense of God, scripture, and our existence. The arguments I've been making support this claim. Perhaps a summary can bring this into focus.

Few theologians consider love their orienting concern. Despite its prominence in the Bible, love has often not functioned as theology's prominent theme. The reasons for this vary. Some scholars seem worried that popular ideas about love are so deeply ingrained that promoting a proper view of love is impossible. Others hold to views of God's predestining, self-centeredness, damnation, and absolute independence that make their love proposals implausible. An idea of divine sovereignty — understood as God controlling or capable of control — conceptually precedes love in many Christian theologies.

Although scripture talks often about love, points to its many forms, and makes a myriad of love claims, biblical writers never define love. At least not concisely or well. This lack of clarity leads to confusion. To make matters worse, the same scriptures that say God *is* love sometimes portray God as unloving. Some passages say God wants violence, revenge, and genocide; others say God may withdraw the love that is supposedly steadfast.

The biblical witness to love is powerful, but not entirely consistent.

I offer a definition of love I think fits the dominant biblical witness. This definition aligns with love as we know it in personal experience and is consonant with contemporary science. In my definition, to love is to act intentionally, in relational response to God and others, to promote overall well-being. This definition applies both to creaturely love and God's love.

Love acts. This action involves deliberation, motives, and freedom, although in varying degrees. Love is relational. Lovers influence others and are influenced by others. God is the relational source of all love, and creatures can love because God first loves them moment by moment. While love often, if not always, includes emotions and desires, it is more than either. Love seeks overall well-being, which means acting for the common good. Love promotes flourishing.

I argue an adequate definition of love proves crucial for constructing an adequate theology of love. Without a good definition, confusion reigns. Without clarity about love's meaning, we cannot identify well the forms of love in scripture and love we express in everyday life.

A clear definition of love proves crucial for understanding central claims of love in the Christian tradition. Statements such as "God loves the world," "love one another," or "love God and neighbor as yourself" require some idea of what "love" means. We also need a definition to make sense of what it means to love enemies, strangers, ourselves, and all creation. Without knowing what love is, we would have no reason to be happy God loves us, and no idea what it means to love like Jesus.

Although love takes various forms, I show each shares the goal of promoting well-being. This means, for instance, that God's love for creation is action that seeks to promote creation's well-being. Loving one another, neighbors, enemies, ourselves, strangers, and all creation means acting to promote overall well-being.

Love's meaning is uniform, but its expressions are pluriform.

In Spite of Obstacles and Difficulties

Among Christians, *agape* is the best known biblical word for love. It's the word New Testament writers use most when speaking of love, human and divine. But *agape* has several meanings in scripture, and it takes many forms. Despite this variety, New Testament writers overwhelmingly use *agape* to describe positive or beneficial action. Love has good motives and aims to promote well-being.

According to scripture writers, love builds up and is generous. It spurs us to humility, patience, and peace. Love nourishes and cherishes; it is kind and forgiving. Love opposes idolatry. It shares with those in need, practices hospitality, feeds the hungry, and gives drink to the thirsty. Love rejoices with those who rejoice and mourns with those who mourn. It blesses instead of curses and tries to live in harmony with others. Loving people will associate with those in low position. Love encourages, helps, and consistently seeks well-being.

We can express love through many practices, according to scripture. We can show love at meals, with kisses, and by warm greetings. Love washes dirty feet and shares with others. It cares for brothers and sisters, the hurting and harmed, for strangers and enemies. Marriage partners should love one another, according to scripture; parents should love children and children should love parents. Love characterizes exemplary leaders and healthy communities. It motivates us to seek healing and to be healing agents for others. Love casts out evil spirits and helps the mentally unstable. Love liberates the oppressed.

Listing every form love takes would be impossible. Writers of scripture could not include every form in their time, and we could not list every form today. Besides those mentioned, we could add others. We can see that love engages in activism, for instance, in the sense of trying to change social patterns and overcome practices that harm. Love encourages artistic expression in many forms. Love tries to protect the vulnerable; it lives in harmony with creation. Love expands our vision of the good life and prompts us to learn how life works. It encourages practical wisdom and self-realization that promotes overall flourishing. And so much more.

To identify *agape* with a general form of love, I suggest it does good in response to enemies, harm, or foreigners. *Agape* does not turn the stranger away but takes the risk of welcome. It does not take revenge; it overcomes evil with good. *Agape* turns the other cheek and responds to curses with blessings. *Agape* promotes, extends, or attempts to establish *shalom* in response to that which promotes sin, evil, and the demonic.

Agape is "in spite of" love, because it seeks good in spite of obstacles and difficulties.

DIVINE AND CREATURELY ACTION

Our exploration of Anders Nygren's theology made clear that theologies of love make claims about who God is, how God acts, and the God-creation relationship. Nygren's theology, however, fails to fit well the biblical witness to love. It also fails to fit our deep intuitions and experiences of love. This is particularly apparent in how Nygren describes divine and creaturely action.

Nygren's failures come partly from his approach to scripture. In his quest to identify *agape* as distinctively Christian, he disregards much of the Old Testament's witness to love. He does not embrace New and Old Testament passages that speak of God's desires and needs. Instead, he considers God absolutely independent and thinks creatures are without intrinsic value. Consequently, Nygren does not embrace biblical statements that say God wants relational friendship with creatures and finds them valuable.

Nygren thinks God controls creatures. In his view, they have no independent power alongside God and make no free choices regarding love. As he sees it, humans are predestined. They are passive tubes through which God loves rather than partners with whom God gives and receives. But if love requires free actions in relation to others, Nygren's theology fails to account for love.

Despite his theology's problems, Nygren affirms that God's nature is love. I say we make best sense of this by saying love is an essential attribute of the divine nature. Love comes logically first in God, which means God must love and we should understand God's other attributes in light of love.

Divine love is unconditional, in the sense that God loves by nature. It is conditional, however, in the sense that divine love takes various forms, depending on the situation and the recipients. God necessarily loves, but freely chooses what forms divine love takes. I call this God's "essence-experience binate," because God's essence of love is unchanging, but God's loving experience changes.

God initiates loving relationship with everyone, all the time. Rather than electing some and predestining others to damnation, God lovingly offers everyone opportunities to love. Creatures can love in any moment because God first loves them.

A theology of pluriform love assumes God is the source of the love creatures express. But being love's source is not the same as being the *only* one capable of love. Nor is it the same as forcing creatures to love. Instead, divine love empowers and inspires through persuasion, and creatures can freely choose whether to love in response.

God loves by nature; creatures choose whether to love.

For Our Sake and God's

Any Christian theology of love should address the thought of Augustine, because his ideas have most affected the development of Christian theology. Augustine considers love primarily as desire, however, not primarily as promoting well-being. Because only God can satisfy our desires, he says, only God deserves our love. We should enjoy and use creatures as means to enjoying the Creator rather than treating them as ends in themselves.

I point out that most Christians overlook or fail to realize the problems that arise when defining love as desire instead of as promoting well-being. There is nothing wrong with desires, of course, and we should prioritize them. But a pluriform theology of love affirms both divine and creaturely desires, and it says love's primary aim is promoting well-being.

One problem with thinking of love as desire emerges when Augustine interprets Jesus' love commands. For Augustine, loving our neighbor as ourselves means loving God *through* our neighbors rather than loving neighbors as ends in themselves. Augustine thinks humans should orient themselves to the unchangeable and perfectly good, which is God, rather than toward what is changeable and not perfectly good. This means, he says, we should not love neighbors or ourselves for our sakes; we must love them for God's sake.

The pluriform theology of love I propose says Jesus' two love commands call us to promote the well-being of neighbors, ourselves, and God. We enjoy and help them for their own sakes, not merely as means to something else. When we love, we can enhance the well-being of God, others, ourselves, and creation.

Problems with Augustine's theology deepen when he explains God's love for the world. God does not love creatures, he says, in the sense of enjoying them. Creatures have nothing valuable to enjoy that God doesn't already have. So God uses creatures, Augustine says, although this is not use as we understand it. He thinks God has no needs, so creatures have nothing God needs to use. When we understand love as desire and conceive of God as only desiring the ultimate good, God cannot love creation in the sense of enjoying, using, or desiring it. God only loves Godself. After looking carefully at Augustine's theology in *Teaching Christianity*, I say Christians should reject his views of love, creaturely and divine.

A pluriform theology of love should adopt *eros*, however, as a particular form of love. Rather than defining *eros* as desire, we might think of it as a form of love that promotes well-being when appreciating what is valuable, worthwhile, or beautiful. *Eros* not only "thinks on" true, honorable, pleasing, and excellent things, it "keeps on doing these things" (Phil. 4:8, 9). Understood this way, God and creatures can express *eros*.

Eros is "because of" love, because it promotes well-being when appreciating values.

ANALOGIES OF LOVE

At the root of Augustine's problems are 1) his view that love is desire rather than action to promote well-being and 2) his doctrine of God. Both problems have strong ties to philosophical ideas common in Augustine's day and that still influence Christian theologians now. Many call the tradition Augustine exemplifies "classical theism." Among other claims, classical theists say God is timeless, immutable, impassible, and simple.

The theology of pluriform love I propose rejects classical theism. Instead of saying God is timeless, it says God experiences the flow of time everlastingly. This makes better sense of God's love as particular divine actions expressed moment by moment. A theology of pluriform love says God's essence is unchanging, but God's experience changes moment by moment. God always loves, because it's God's nature to do so, but God's love influences creatures and creatures influence God in response. God is relational rather than impassible. A theology of pluriform love says God is unified rather than simple in the sense that God's actions, attributes, and existence are identical.

Classical theism's assumptions make it difficult, if not impossible, to talk about God as loving. It considers divine love entirely different from creaturely love. Because of this radical dissimilarity, classical theism cannot support analogies between God and creation. The classical God shares no likeness with creatures, has no relations with self or others, and does not act in any way creatures know as acting. The classical God has no emotions in relation to creation and needs no one.

Classical theism's claims about divine love often, if not always, end up in appeals to absolute mystery. While we will never understand love fully, appeals to absolute mystery are not supported by biblical claims about God's love. Saying "God loves the world," "God is love," or that we should imitate God's love makes absolutely no sense if God's love is absolutely mysterious.

God's love cannot be altogether different in kind from our love.

I suggest seven analogies that point to similarities and differences between the love God and creatures express. These analogies align with themes in scripture and provide language to talk coherently about love. I suggest both Creator and creatures give and receive in loving relationship, but only God does so perfectly, and only God relates to all others. Both Creator and creatures love in the ongoing flow of time, but only God loves everlastingly. Both Creator and creatures love by promoting overall well-being, but only God promotes well-being directly to everything in the universe. Both creatures and Creator love as experiencers, but only God feels the emotional tones of every creature. Both Creator and creatures love freely, but creatures can choose not to love. God necessarily loves. Both creatures and Creator have needs, but to exist, God does not rely upon creatures, whereas creatures rely upon God for their existence. Both Creator and creatures are valuable in themselves, but God is supremely valuable.

These analogies of similarity and difference provide grounds to say God transcends creation in some ways but is immanent in others. If God were altogether transcendent, claims about divine love would be meaningless. If God were altogether immanent, claims about divine love would not differ from claims about creaturely love. To make sense of love in scripture and our experience, an adequate theology points to differences, but also similarities between Creator and creatures.

The Promise of Open and Relational Theology

Open and relational theology offers a helpful framework for a theology of pluriform love. Although diverse, this theological movement embraces the idea that God gives and receives in relation to creatures and creation. So conceived, God moves through time like creatures do, experiencing moment by moment. Open and relational theologians typically embrace creaturely freedom, the intrinsic value of creation, experience as fundamental, love as central to God's nature, and love as the aim for creatures.

Clark Pinnock offers a winsome version of Christian open and relational theology. His views not only align with the broad biblical witness, but also account for relational themes present in human experience. God inspires free creatures to love, says Pinnock. Rather than being immobile and impassible, the God Pinnock describes engages in mutually influencing relationships with creation. I believe that those constructing a Christian theology of love should adopt most of Pinnock's views.

But besides embracing open and relational views about God and creation like Pinnock's, my theology of pluriform love focuses especially upon Jesus. Jesus reveals divine love in powerful ways. In his life, teachings, ministry, death, and resurrection, Jesus enacts the way of love. He healed the sick, preached good news, was a friend to sinners, ministered to the poor, wept over the dead, encouraged the downhearted, partied with celebrants, and showed compassion. His death highlights God's suffering and that God wants to save all. Jesus' resurrection provides hope of continuing life and love after bodily death.

Christians would be wise to follow Jesus' example. This not only means loving in communities of common cause, but it also means loving strangers, enemies, themselves, all creation, and God. Jesus' life inaugurated new ways of existing and new communities of followers. In him are light and life and love.

Jesus Christ is the center of a Christian theology that makes love central.

Jesus' kenotic love provides a solution to the problem of evil. His love was not overpowering or coercive; it was self-giving and others-empowering. Jesus was humble, servant-like, self-sacrificial, and looked not only to himself but also to the common good. He embodied *kenosis*.

Jesus' revelation of love suggests God is essentially kenotic. I argue that rather than being deliberately self-limiting, God essentially self-gives and others-empowers. I call this "essential kenosis." It claims that because God loves everyone and everything, God cannot control anyone or anything. Divine love is uncontrolling.

Essential Kenosis and Evil

Most Christian theologies fail to address well the primary reason many people do not think God loves perfectly or does not exist at all. That reason: the evil we experience personally and witness every day in the world. People rightly wonder why a powerful and loving God doesn't prevent pointless pain and unnecessary suffering.

The usual answers given to the problem of evil fail. They may contain a kernel of truth, but they do not answer well our central questions. I believe it's impossible to portray a God of perfect love if we also say God could prevent genuine evil but fails to do so. A God who wants, causes, or even permits pointless pain is not a God who loves everyone and everything all the time. Skeptics rightly reject theologies of love that do not solve the problem of evil.

Traditional views of divine power are the root of most failures to account for evil. But we can solve the prominent dimensions of the problem of evil if we embrace essential kenosis. This view says God necessarily self-gives to and others-empowers everyone and everything, which means God cannot control anyone or anything. The God who cannot control cannot prevent evil singlehandedly.

Rethinking God's power as uncontrolling allows a theology of pluriform love to say that God is not culpable for causing or allowing evil. This uncontrolling God suffers with those who suffer, however, and works to heal creatures and creation. God does not abandon the harmed and hurting, but works with them to squeeze something good from bad. God calls creatures to join in the work of overcoming evil with good through indispensable love synergy.

The God of uncontrolling, pluriform love opposes evil.

Classical theism's grip on Christian theology is so strong that claiming God's love is uncontrolling will strike many as unorthodox. To many Christians, a God who cannot control must be limited. But biblical writers and leading theologians say there are many things God cannot do. Essential kenosis adds that divine love is uncontrolling. But this does not mean God is limited in any coherent way, any more than other types of limitation we already accept.

Christian theologies that make love a priority require new conceptions of divine power. These concepts should fit the primary witness of scripture and Jesus' witness to kenotic love. Both witnesses suggest God is neither omnipotent *nor* impotent. I recommend saying God is "amipotent:" divine power is the power of love. As One mightier than any other, exerting might upon all others, and the source of might for all others, God's almighty influence is uncontrolling love.

Essential Hesed and Unfaithfulness

The Old Testament's witness to love is powerful. Although scholars translate several Hebrew words as love or something similar, *ahavah* and *hesed* are the most prominent. *Ahavah* usually describes the care, attachment, and affection lovers show to others. According to biblical writers, God expresses *ahavah* for creatures and creation. This biblical witness aligns with open and relational theology's view that God is relational, has desires, and experiences emotions.

Biblical scholars translate *hesed* in various ways, including "covenantal love," "loyal faithfulness," and "steadfast love." According to scripture, God expresses *hesed* by helping, being generous, and doing good. Those faithful in covenant enjoy health, meaningful life, and well-being. The covenantal love of *hesed* fits the open and relational vision, because it assumes God is influenced and does not know with certainty what creatures will do in response to covenant.

"The steadfast love of the Lord endures forever" is a recurring theme in the Old Testament. God's everlasting love provides well-being. God makes covenants with particular persons, Israel, other nations, and all creation. Because divine *hesed* is everlasting and universal, we can count on God's faithful goodness.

We have good reasons to say *hesed* is essential to God. Divine *hesed* is unconditional, in the sense that God loves, and creatures did not earn this love. This corresponds with the idea God is essentially loving. How God chooses to express *hesed* varies, however. This is another way to affirm God's essence-experience binate.

Creatures are not always faithful. But God is no creature; God cannot be unfaithful. I call this "essential hesed." It says God is necessarily faithful, which means God cannot leave us, cannot forsake us, always suffers with us, always empathizes, always accepts, and is essentially *for* creation.

Essential hesed says the covenantal God faithfully loves.

A pluriform theology of love offers hope and security to people who feel hopeless and abandoned. The always present, always caring, and faithful Friend can be counted on to do good and never desert us. The God of essential *hesed* is everlastingly faithful to everyone and all creation.

It's difficult to worship a God who loves half-heartedly. We can't worship a God whose love makes no sense. A being like this would be neither perfect nor praiseworthy. But the God of essential hesed and essential kenosis loves uncontrollingly, wholeheartedly, and faithfully. We can trust a God who is in no sense culpable and always seeks well-being.

It makes sense to connect love and worship if our actions can enhance God's well-being. We can desire God, in the sense of wanting God's direction and appreciating God's glory, and we can love God, in the sense of blessing God in praise and adoration. Our praise and worship enhance our well-being and God's; creation and Creator benefit.

We can worship without reservation the God of uncontrolling love.

God, in Love, Everlastingly Creates in Relation to Creation

If God steadfastly loves creation forever, there must *always* be creation to love. We should reject the idea God once existed alone and reject the idea God creates from absolutely nothing. As we have seen, the Bible does not explicitly endorse those ideas. Rejecting them allows us to say God never used controlling power and cannot create from nothing to prevent genuine evil.

The doctrine of *creatio ex nihilo* directly and indirectly renders God culpable for evil. The God who created our universe from nothing would be responsible for the possibilities of evil. This God could instantaneously create from nothing obstacles to evil in the present, but doesn't do so, leading to moral incoherence.

Creatio ex nihilo also implies God is essentially solitary and not essentially related to creation. A God not essentially related to creatures does not essentially love them; that God is independent by nature. If we want to say love for creation is God's nature and the steadfast love of the Lord endures forever, we need an alternative creation doctrine.

In the name of love, we should reject *creatio ex nihilo*.

I propose a new creation theory that says God, in love, everlastingly creates out of or in relation to creation. We might render it in Latin as *creatio ex creatione sempiternalis in amore*. God's motive for creating is love, and God uses materials God previously created. God always creates alongside creatures, who are created co-creators. And God never controls when creating, because divine love is necessarily uncontrolling. A theology of pluriform love places love as the center of its doctrine of creation.

New theories are often misunderstood. To clarify, my theory does not say our universe is eternal. It had a beginning, likely as a Big Bang, but another universe preceded it. Nor does my theory say creaturely "stuff" predates God. God creates all creatures and creations. *Creatio ex creatione sempiternalis in amore* does not make God's existence dependent upon creation. God exists necessarily and necessarily creates alongside others. My theory denies an eternal dualism between good and evil and denies God creates out of Godself. It does not say God simply rearranges what already exists; God always creates something new.

We might call the God who always, in love, creates out of what God previously created the "Ever Creator." Creating is an aspect of God's essential nature. But an open and relational God freely chooses *how* and *what* to create, given creaturely conditions and God's own nature of love. Unlike the God of classical theism, creating is what the God of essential hesed always does, because it's God's nature to be Creator.

Alongside of Love

An open and relational theology of pluriform love emphasizes themes of collaboration, cooperation, and mutuality. Love's aims require both Creator and creatures. The reign of love is not possible by divine fiat, nor is it possible through creaturely effort alone. Love requires co-operating and co-laboring.

The relational dimensions of *hesed* fit nicely with *philia*, a Greek word New Testament writers sometimes use to describe both divine and creaturely love. As a form of love, I say that *philia* acts intentionally, in relational response to God and others, to promote overall well-being through cooperation and friendship. It co-labors in seeking good. *Philia* is companion love.

I call *philia* the "alongside of" form of love. This alongside of dimension, over time, leads to the qualities we identify with friendship. Creatures can enjoy friendship love with their Creator and other creatures, which means God's experience and the experience of creatures can be enhanced. The God of essential *hesed* consistently expresses and seeks *philia* as creation's everlasting Friend.

God's inability to control creation and the reality of an open future mean that for love to win, God relies upon creatures. This reliance means creatures and creaturely choices *really* matter. Classical theologies assume the end has already been determined or God can determine it unilaterally. In such scenarios, our lives and choices don't ultimately count. But a theology of pluriform love says God can't control, and it provides a foundation to affirm ultimate significance for creaturely lives and actions.

What we do makes a difference to God and to the future.

Pluriform Love

Most Christian theologies restrict divine love. According to many, God only expresses *agape*. According to others, God only expresses *eros*. Some theologies may say God expresses *hesed* but cannot affirm divine *ahavah*. Other theologians mix and match loves, depending on their philosophical and theological assumptions.

The theology I propose says God expresses *agape, eros, philia, kenosis, ahavah, hesed*, and more. Divine love is pluriform. The biblical witness, the history of creation, and our lives bear witness to God at work in wild and wonderful ways. Our imitating God requires that we express pluriform love. The diversity of love forms to which God calls fills a lifetime of enjoying and sharing abundant life.

To illustrate visually how I understand the definition of love as uniform but its expressions as pluriform, I offer the figure below. Note that some forms mentioned are quite broad, while others are fairly specific.

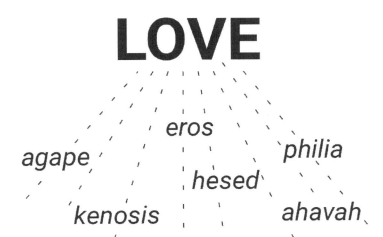

enemy love	stranger love	self-love	friendship love
self-sacrificial love	compassion	sex/romance love	family love
protective love	activist love	artistic love	hospitality love
forgiving love	love of nature	playful love	love of community
healing love	liberative love	caregiving love	partying love
suffering love	philanthropic love	self-improving love	love of nation

There are millions more forms of love than I list. And many forms mix with others. For instance, I can both love my daughter appreciating her value and love her by expressing my disappointment that she made an unhealthy decision. I can act for my nation's well-being in collaboration with others while actively opposing policies the majority seem to adopt. And so on. God's love is mixed too. God both loves by appreciating the value of creatures while loving in anger when they abuse one another.

Rather than one-dimensional, God's love is pluriform.

God loves creation in at least three primary ways. First, God acts for creation's good, even when creatures harm themselves and others. God loves even when we are unfaithful to God and sin. God's love takes the form of acting for good in spite of the negative that creatures have done. As a forgiving lover, God expresses *agape*.

Second, God acts for creation's good when encountering its intrinsic value. This form of divine love does good because of the beauty, worth, and importance of creation. The world God created and creates is good. As an artistic lover, God expresses *eros*.

Third, God loves by coming alongside creatures in the work of promoting well-being. God empowers and seeks collaboration from creation for the common good. As a loving friend, God expresses *philia*.

Each broad form of divine love takes various expressions. But in each, God seeks to promote well-being.

Relentless Love

If the steadfast love of the Lord endures forever, it does not end when we die. God loves us in the afterlife too. Divine love is relentless.[1]

In the opening chapters, I said an adequate theology of love denies that a loving God sends anyone to hell. A loving person would not condemn another to eternal conscious torment. Divine love,

---

[1] I explain my view of the afterlife and relentless love in several books. See, for instance, *Questions and Answers for God Can't*, ch. 8.

as the Apostle Paul puts it, "always hopes" and "never ends" (1 Cor. 13:7,8), even after we leave these mortal coils.

A loving God doesn't suddenly take up coercion in the afterlife, of course, or force everyone to experience heavenly bliss. God's love remains uncontrolling in the afterlife too. God continues to invite every creature capable of responding to enjoy the well-being love provides. God is the everlasting beckoner.

Creatures who cooperate with God's invitation flourish. They enjoy the natural positive consequences that come from embracing God's gift of well-being. But creatures now and in the afterlife can choose not to cooperate. When they do, they suffer the natural negative consequences that come from choosing something other than well-being. As the Apostle John puts it, we pass "from death to life because we love one another." But John adds that "whoever does not love abides in death" (1 Jn. 3:14). I take "death" here to point to negative natural consequences and "life" to positive ones.

A loving God doesn't punish, and God always forgives. But creatures who choose something other than love choose something other than well-being. They hurt themselves and others.

The God of relentless love never gives up. Ever. While creatures can say "No" to God now and in the afterlife, God everlastingly invites all to live lives of love. Because of relentless love, we have grounds to hope all will eventually say "Yes." Everlasting persuasive love makes it possible for everyone to experience everlasting bliss.

Relentless love reminds us that love for creation isn't a temporary experiment on God's part. Love for creation is God's heart, nature, or essence. And because of divine amipotence, we can imagine the Apostle Paul's vision — that all creation be redeemed (Rom. 8:20-22) — becoming a reality.

Conclusion

I began this book by saying it's not hard to argue love stands at the center of the biblical witness. Consequently, I argued, love should be the center of Christian theology. In the chapters that followed, I've pointed to obstacles that prevent Christians from embracing love. I've provided a theology that makes scripture's witness to love central and that takes seriously our own experiences of love.

"…and the greatest of these is love," says Paul to conclude his love hymn (1 Cor. 13:13b). By defining love, exploring influential theologians, and identifying love's forms, I offer a Christian theology of pluriform love.

Immediately after saying, "the greatest of these is love," Paul tells his readers to "pursue love" (1 Cor. 14:1a). A conceptual framework for making sense of love, in general, and for understanding God's love, in particular, helps us acknowledge love's preeminence and pursue love with joy.

Thanks to God's pluriform love, we can receive and express pluriform love.

For the remainder of this book, visit your favorite bookseller...

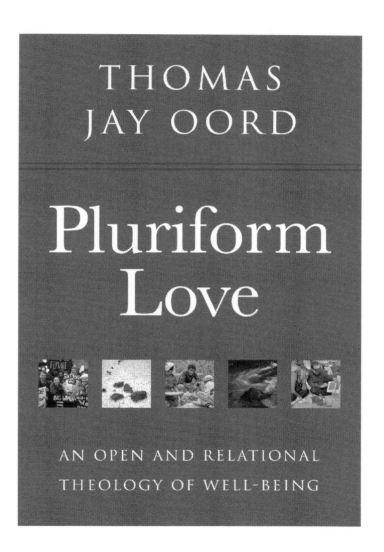

THOMAS
JAY OORD

Pluriform
Love

AN OPEN AND RELATIONAL
THEOLOGY OF WELL-BEING

Information on Thomas Jay Oord

Thomas Jay Oord, Ph.D., is a theologian, philosopher, and scholar of multi-disciplinary studies. Oord directs the Center for Open and Relational Theology and doctoral students at Northwind Theological Seminary. He is an award-winning and best-selling author who has written or edited more than thirty books. A gifted speaker, Oord lectures at universities, conferences, churches, seminaries, and institutions. A world-renown theologian of love, Oord also is known for his research in science and religion, open and relational theology, the problem of suffering, and the implications of freedom for transformational relationships.

For information, see Dr. Oord's website: thomasjayoord.com

For information on the Open and Relational Theology doctoral program Dr. Oord directs, see northwindseminary.org/center-for-open-relational-theology

For information on the Center for Open and Relational Theology, see c4ort.com

Books Written or Edited by Thomas Jay Oord

Pluriform Love: An Open and Relational Theology. Grasmere, Id.: SacraSage, 2022.

Open and Relational Theology: An Introduction to Life-Changing Ideas. Grasmere, Id.: SacraSage, 2021.

Partnering with God: Exploring Collaboration in Open and Relational Theology. Edited with Bonnie Rambob, Tim Reddish, and Fran Stedman. Grasmere, Id.: SacraSage, 2021.

Questions and Answers for God Can't. Grasmere, Id.: SacraSage Press, 2020.

Open and Relational Leadership: Leading with Love. Edited with Roland Hearn and Sheri D. Kling. Grasmere, Id.: SacraSage Press, 2020.

God Can't! How to Believe in God and Love after Tragedy, Abuse, and Other Evils. SacraSage, 2019. Spanish Translation: *Dio No Puede: Como Creer en Dios y el Amor Despues de la Tragedia, el Abuso y Otros Males,* Lemuel Sandoval, trans. (2019). German Translation, German Translation: *GOTT kann das nicht! Wie man trotz Tragödien, Missbrauch oder anderem Unheil den Glauben an Gott und Seine Liebe bewahrt,* Michael Trenkel and Dirk Weisensee, trans. (SacraSage, 2020).

Women Experiencing Faith. Edited with Janel Apps Ramsey. Grasmere, ID: SacraSage, 2018.

Rethinking the Bible: Inerrancy, Preaching, Inspiration, Authority, Formation, Archaeology, Postmodernism, and More. Grasmere, ID: SacraSage, 2018.

Theologians and Philosophers Using Social Media: Advice, Tips, and Testimonials. Edited. San Diego: SacraSage, 2017.

The Uncontrolling Love of God: An Open and Relational Theology of Providence. Downers Grove, Ill: Intervarsity, 2015. Portuguese Translation: *O Amor Nao Control Ador de Deus,* 2020. German Translation: *Gottes Liebe zwingt nicht: Ein offener und relationaler Zugang zum Wirken Gottes in der Welt.* Matthias Remenyi, Foreword; Julia Nöthling and Felix Fleckenstein, Translators, 2020.

Through Both Creations Shine. Blurb, 2015.

Renovating Holiness. Edited with Josh Broward. Boise: SacraSage, 2015.

Theologies of Creation: Creatio ex Nihilo and Its New Rivals. Editor and contributor. New York: Routledge, 2014.

Nazarenes Exploring Evolution. Edited with Sherri Walker. Boise: SacraSage, 2013.

Relational Theology: A Contemporary Introduction. Edited with Brint Montgomery and Karen Winslow. San Diego: Point Loma University Press, 2012.

The Bible Tells Me So: Reading the Bible as Scripture. Edited with Richard Thompson. SacraSage, 2011.

God in an Open Universe: Science, Metaphysics, and Open Theism. Editor with William Hasker and Dean Zimmerman. Eugene, OR: Pickwick Press, 2011.

The Best News You Will Ever Hear. With Robert Luhn. Boise, ID: Elevate, 2011. Spanish Translation: *Las Mejores Noticias que Escucharas,* 2012.

The Polkinghorne Reader. London: SPCK Press; Philadelphia: Templeton Foundation Press, 2010.

The Nature of Love: A Theology. St. Louis, Mo.: Chalice Press, 2010.

Defining Love: A Philosophical, Scientific, and Theological Engagement. Grand Rapids, Mich.: Brazos, 2010.

Divine Grace and Emerging Creation: Wesleyan Forays in Science and Theology of Creation. Editor and Contributor. Eugene, OR: Pickwick, 2009.

Love Among Us. Edited with Darrin Grinder. Denver, Colo.: Outskirts Press, 2009.

Postmodern and Wesleyan: Exploring the Boundaries and the Possibilities. Editor with Jay Akkerman and Brent Peterson. Kansas City, Mo.: Beacon Hill Press, 2009.

Creation Made Free: Open Theology and Science. Editor and contributor. Eugene: Pickwick, 2009.

The Altruism Reader: Selections from Writings on Love, Religion and Science. Philadelphia: Templeton Foundation Press, 2008.

The Many Facets of Love: Philosophical Explorations. Editor and Contributor. Cambridge: Cambridge Scholars Press, 2007.

Relational Holiness: Responding to the Call of Love, with Michael Lodahl. Kansas City: Beacon Hill Press, 2005. Spanish Translation: *Santidad Relacional: Respuesta al llamado de amor* (Venezuela, 2006). Dutch Translation, Ank Verhoeven: *Ons antwoord op Gods liefde: Een relationele kijk op heiliging* (SacraSage, 2021).

Science of Love: The Wisdom of Well-Being. Philadelphia: Templeton Press, 2004. Spanish translation: *La cience del Amor. Sabiduria del bienestar* (Mexico: Panorama, 2006). Polish translation: *Milosc: Sprawai, Ze Swiat Sie Kreci: naukaow o milosci* (Krakow, Poland: Wydawnictwo WAM, 2009).

Philosophy of Religion: Essay Introductions. Editor and contributor. Kansas City, Mo.: Beacon Hill Press, 2003.

Thy Name and Thy Nature is Love: Wesleyan and Process Theologies in Dialogue. Editor, with Bryan P. Stone. Nashville: Kingswood, 2001.

TO READ
Thomas Jay Oord...

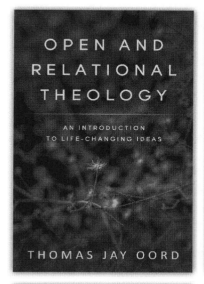

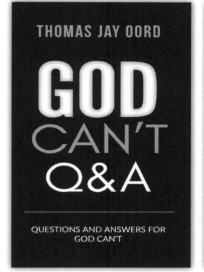

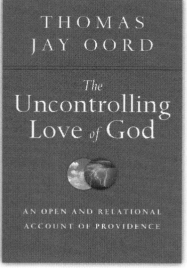

TO READ
Thomas Jay Oord...

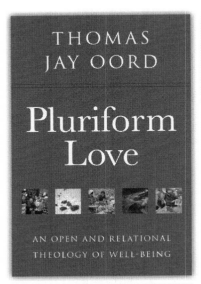

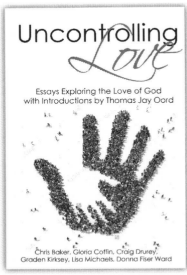

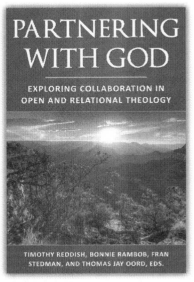

Made in the USA
Middletown, DE
18 August 2023

36465525R00135